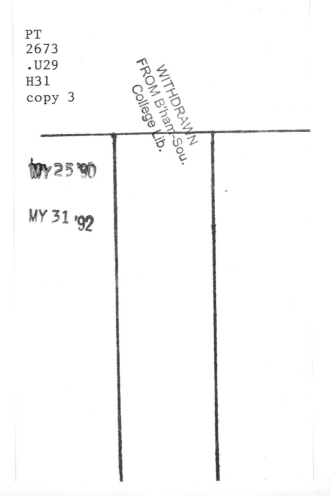

Hamletmachine
and
Other Texts for the Stage

❧ ❧

Heiner Müller

Edited and Translated by Carl Weber

Performing Arts Journal Publications
New York

Library of Congress Cataloging in Publication Data
Hamletmachine and Other Texts for the Stage
Library of Congress Catalog Card No.: 83-61193
ISBN: 0-933826-44-3 (cloth)
ISBN: 0-933826-45-1 (paper)

Printed in the United States of America

Publication of this book has been made possible in part by grants received from the National Endowment for the Arts, Washington, D.C., a federal agency, and the New York State Council on the Arts.

General Editors of the PAJ Playscript Series:
Bonnie Marranca and Gautam Dasgupta

Contents

Preface

It is a privilege to present a first collection of texts by Heiner Müller to American readers interested in drama, in the performing arts, and in their interaction with history. Heiner Müller is recognized as one of the most important and controversial playwrights of our time—not only in the four countries speaking his tongue but in the rest of Europe as well. There have been productions of his plays in the U.S.—in Austin, Berkeley, San Francisco and New York—yet, aside from his reputation among scholars of German literature and contemporary drama, Heiner Müller is virtually unknown in this country. I hope this edition will create the interest his work so richly deserves.

******

It was no easy task to select the texts for this volume: Müller has written more than twenty-five plays and pieces for performance, several adaptations, some short stories, poetry, and numerous essays and articles on the theatre and its function in our time. In 1975/76, he visited the U.S. for an extended period, and travelled widely here and in Mexico. This visit marked the end of one phase of his work, or better—the beginnings of a new approach. Until 1975, his work was exclusively concerned with problems important and indigenous to his native country and to the developing "Real Socialism" in the German Democratic Republic, whatever particular period or mythological disguise he decided to present his topics in. After his return to Europe in 1976, his work began to explore new directions, his perspective transcended Central Europe to focus on problems of world-wide social and political dimensions, while in his dramaturgy he increasingly made use of the innovations experimental theatre in the West had introduced.

It seemed a logical choice to present in this first edition to be published in America all of the plays he wrote since 1976, when he first visited this country. It offers a body of work which spans an amazing spectrum of topics, styles, genres, and dramaturgical techniques. On the other hand, I felt it useful to indicate at least some of the stations in his long and complicated growth as a playwright. I included one of his earliest pieces, THE CORRECTION (1957), to serve as an example of how much Muller owes to Brecht whose models he adopted and developed over a period of twenty years. He indeed became the only playwright of his generation in Germany who was acclaimed as the successor to Brecht. My second choice written before 1975 is MEDEAPLAY (1974). It was his first published exploration of a theatre of images after two decades spent in refining his use of poetic language for the stage. His skills as a poet and the power of his language were further reasons why many critics claimed Brecht's mantle for Müller.

******

The introduction tries as much as possible to let Müller speak for himself, by way of quotes from discussions and interviews, and occasional excerpts from his writings. It is not intended to be a scholarly analysis but a first "guided tour" through his complex work and life. Both should be great stuff for academic research and learned investigation, and Müller has indeed become a favorite subject for European critics and scholars of theatre and literature.

******

I'd like to thank Bonnie Marranca and Gautam Dasgupta, the editors and publishers of Performing Arts Journal Publications, for their courage in publishing this book, and for their support and neverfailing belief in our project.

My special gratitude belongs to Michael Roloff; his help and advice on the translations has been invaluable. Without his friendship this would have been a lesser book.

And last, not least, I thank my wife Marianne for her encouragement and her understanding.

C.W.

HEINER MÜLLER

The Pressure of Experience

Performance artist Robert Wilson is creating one of his huge spectacles for the 1984 Olympic Games in Los Angeles, in which artists from all over the world will participate, writing, composing, or performing for this ambitious venture, entitled *the CIVIL warS*. Among the names announced as collaborators are David Bowie and Philip Glass, David Byrne, Hildegard Behrens, Gavin Bryars, and an East German playwright and poet few people this side of the Atlantic had ever heard of—Heiner Müller.

At the 1983 Holland Festival ten companies from five countries were invited to The Hague to present nine plays during a special "Heiner Müller Festival." Not all of these productions were to be seen, though; the companies from Müller's own country were refused permission by the GDR authorities to travel to Holland, one of them Berlin's Volksbühne, which was to perform Müller's own production of his play MACBETH.

These incidents, in all their controversial aspects, indicate that Heiner Müller is acknowledged as an important playwright of our time; they also emphasize that his work and his positions are inseparable from the schizophrenia of today's partitioned Germany.

Müller is one of the few dramatists today who could be called a "universal playwright," a playwright asking questions and expressing traumas that concern all of contemporary mankind, not only one group, nation, class or culture. This may sound quite grandiose, yet Müller's vision is not a microscopic view. He observes man as if from another planet, through an immensely powerful telescope. He writes with the hope that what he calls "a universal history of man" is eventually going to begin, setting his utopia against the reality of universal misery he sees everywhere.

He grew up as a Marxist, first under Fascist oppression, then in a Socialist system he strongly believed in. Today, it seems he is becoming increasingly doubtful that a linear concept of history as Marx, and before him Hegel, constructed it can encompass and/or define the complex situation contemporary mankind finds itself in. Yet, he is convinced that Communism, not necessarily the "Real Socialism" of the present Eastern bloc, remains as the only hope left, that our race will destroy itself and, maybe, the planet it inhabits if it continues to pursue the present political and social course. As he wrote of his last play, DESPOILED SHORE MEDEAMATERIAL LANDSCAPE WITH ARGONAUTS: ". . . it presumes the catastrophes which mankind is working toward. The theatre's contribution to their prevention can only be their representation."

Müller's "relatives" in the contemporary theatre are few. One could name Beckett, Genet and Edward Bond. Müller's last plays could certainly be called "endgames"; his MACBETH is close to Edward Bond's view of *Lear*; and THE TASK, even more, QUARTET show his affinity to Genet, about whom he said: "I believe that Genet articulated very precisely and correctly: The only thing a work of art can achieve is to create the desire for a different state of the world. And this desire is revolutionary." (Müller in an interview for *Der Spiegel*, May 9, 1983.)

None of this proves that Heiner Müller should by necessity find his place on the American stage. As long as a playwright fails to investigate aspects of life that are burning issues for a nation or a culture, he can at best become a most interesting, yet somewhat exotic, author to be studied by scholars and critics of the theatre. However, Muller is writing about issues which should concern—deeply concern—our society. To name only two: the role of the intellectual as an opinion-maker, and the terrible distance which separates even the most liberal and progressive member of a colonizing system from its colonized victims. It is certainly no accident that these two subjects moved to the center of his work after he visited the U.S., the first time as a writer-in-residence at the University of Texas in Austin, 1975, and later for an extended stay in 1978/79.

Comparison of his works written before and after his travels shows clearly how the experience of America altered his perception of the world. Among other things, his view of nature changed. If nature was barely of any importance in his earlier work, "landscape" is an increasingly important topic now. In a radio interview for *Deutschlandfunk*, April 9, 1982, Müller remarked: "What was new to me was the discovery that a landscape can be a political phenomenon, and that I can have a relation to landscapes, simply because of the dimensions of those landscapes over there. And because of the fact that they never can become quite domesticated. There always remains something more. Then, I found very interesting what enormous free spaces are produced by this sort of Capitalism on its fringes, simply fringes where enormous values are wasted because they aren't negotiable, aren't marketable. In these fringes a lot of things can move. The Federal Republic or Switzerland are well-groomed front lawns compared with [the U.S.]. This archaic, even anarchistic, feature of [American] Capitalism I found very interesting."

He also observed the contorted and awkward stance of many American intellectuals and "opinion-makers" desperately trying to straddle the contradictions of an exploitative system that, while granting them all the freedoms, relegates them to a position of impotence. Once, when I asked him if HAMLETMACHINE wouldn't be difficult to understand for American audiences without the experience of European post-war history, he replied: "The general, objective situation isn't that different here. As an intellectual [in the U.S.] you belong at last to the middle class; as soon as you even make the beginnings of a career, as you have some success, you belong to the establishment you fight against. You get into the establishment by fighting it; as a writer of literature, for instance, there is no other way to join it, I believe. But then you're 'in' and live in the dilemma that you belong, yet don't like to. And it's quite typical here that once very good authors have written a best-seller, their tragedy of success begins; people are ground down by success."

Of course, the German intellectual who castrates himself deliberately, as he appears in Lenz/Brecht's play *The Tutor* for instance, had always been familiar to Müller. After all, he had suffered from the "tutors" of his own country from the time he began to write for the stage.

In his way, Heiner Müller defends the victimized individual oppressed by the forces of modern industrial society more aggressively than most contemporary playwrights, even as he anticipates the defeat and final disappearance of the individual in this struggle, declaring that "the individual subject doesn't interest me anymore." He focuses a pitiless and deep-cutting stare at all our assumptions about the individual and the society in which he lives, at the forces that mold human society, and the history that propelled mankind towards its present, perhaps doomed, state. This harsh view, and the "pessimistic" stance he often has been accused of, have to be seen against the background of Central European history.

Heiner Müller is very much a son of his nation, and the obsessions and traumas inflicted on the German people—and inflicted by them on others— have become his own. The German "split"; the "two souls dwelling in my breast" the archetypal German, Dr. Faustus, agonizes over; Hamlet,—"this 'very German' character," as Muller once said—torn apart by the contradictions of existence; the divided Germany of today's political map—no other German writer represents these schisms as boldly and clearly in his life and work. This "schizophrenia" is one, if not the most important, reason why Müller lives in East Berlin while freely using his privilege to travel to the West whenever he pleases, a privilege he feels guilty about at the same time. He explained his position in the *Der Spiegel* interview quoted earlier:

> Q.: Haven't you lived already some time in the no-man's-land between the two German states?
>
> H.M.: Of course, this back and forth between two very different German realities has a schizophrenic effect. The GDR is important to me because all the dividing lines of our world go through this country. That's the true state of the world and it has become quite "concrete" in the Berlin Wall. There exists a much greater "pressure of experience" in the GDR than here [in West Germany] and that's of interest to me professionally: the pressure of experience as a pre-condition of writing. Life is more obliging on the Eastern side of the Wall and that also constitutes the compulsion to think everything through radically to its end, to formulate everything to its end, while here you still can play around it."

Thinking radically, investigating the social and historical trends of our world to their final, if lethal, consequence: these are the tasks that concern Heiner Müller. Once he articulated his experience of "writing radically": "My pen sometimes 'resists' the text I force it to put on paper." This statement reveals that the process of writing has become more and more an integral part of the result, which is incorporated in Müller's texts. He doesn't believe anymore in keeping himself, the writer, outside of his texts in a detached position. This is nowhere more evident than in HAMLETMACHINE when the photo of the author is torn on stage. Yet, it is also a central aspect of the portrait of a writer in LESSING'S SLEEP DREAM SCREAM, or of LANDSCAPE WITH ARGONAUTS. Müller explained in 1978: "A phase has ended for me. I have to find a new approach now. The historical substance has been used up for me from the vantage point I tried to employ while writing about it . . . You can't come to grips with the macro-structures [of society] anymore by way of literature. Now the problem is the micro-structure . . . The author can't ignore himself anymore . . . If I don't talk about myself I'll reach no one anymore."

Tearing his own photo in HAMLETMACHINE was a forceful way of talking about himself, a powerful metaphor for the author's view of himself. When asked about this "new approach" in the *Deutschlandfunk* interview quoted earlier, Müller specified: "At bottom, playwriting always means to me that a picture is torn, a picture of myself too. In one play one picture is torn, from this a new picture originates. And that has to be torn again. That is actually the process." This never ceasing re-assessment, a constant probing of his experience and its implications, has become increasingly important in Müller's writing since he visited America.

******

In a discussion with Sylvere Lotringer published 1982 in *Semiotext(e)*, Müller remarked: "I'm always in a difficult situation when I'm forced to interpret my own writings. I write more than I know. I write in another time than the one I'm living in." This statement is a far cry from the opinions held by the young journalist and budding author of the early fifties who was an ardent admirer of Brecht, and eventually became the German dramatist who was called "a successor of Brecht," with good reason. Lately Müller has defined his position in contrast to Brecht—tongue in cheek—using the term "parricide," in a panel discussion at a conference of the International Brecht Society, held May 1979 at the University of Maryland, College Park.

Müller's early plays, of which THE CORRECTION (1957) in this volume is a sample, were written in the Epic mode Brecht had established. Müller emulated ideas Brecht discussed in his last years, designs for a theatre Brecht liked to call "Dialectic Theatre," a dramaturgy replacing the earlier "Epic Theatre." Müller's first plays could also be considered as pieces for "a new, operative form of Agitprop-Theatre" that Brecht so insistently encouraged in the mid-fifties. Anyone familiar with Brecht's work, especially his writings on theatre and his directorial achievements at the Berliner Ensemble, will recognize the influence when reading THE CORRECTION. Yet, as closely as the play follows an Epic dramaturgy, some of its structural features point to tendencies in Müller's later work that didn't come fully to the fore until the mid-seventies; some short pieces, fragmentary scenes like THE SHEET, he wrote early in the fifties and didn't publish until twenty years later as part of the text THE BATTLE, also tried to transcend the Brechtian model.

However, until and including the play CEMENT (1972), Müller employed in most respects a dramaturgy that was a development and extrapolation of Brecht's structures, even when he introduced some far reaching and important innovations within this framework, for instance in MAUSER (1970), his treatment of a theme from Brecht's *Die Massnahme (The Measures Taken)*. GERMANIA DEATH IN BERLIN (1971) was his first leap out of the confinements of Brecht's model and towards the new form of the "synthetic fragment," as Müller later called it. Seemingly disparate scenes, or parts of scenes, are combined without any particular effort at a coherent, linear plot. The result is a kind of assemblage, much like a not yet fully structured work-in-progress, such as Georg Buchner's fragment *Woyzeck*, for example. Müller's "fragments," of course, are painstakingly crafted texts, "synthesized" from often widely diverse constituents, as GUND-LING'S LIFE FREDERICK OF PRUSSIA LESSING'S SLEEP DREAM SCREAM, HAMLETMACHINE, THE TASK, and DESPOILED SHORE MEDEAMATERIAL LANDSCAPE WITH ARGONAUTS attest. This is a dramatic structure, or rather anti-structure, he has developed and refined to arrive at a dramaturgy which could be defined as "post-structuralist" or "deconstructionist."

All this labelling has to be taken with some caution. Müller defies labels others try to pin on him. He never ceases to surprise his critics and to baffle his audiences. Again and again he has disowned statements he made in the past, happily admitting that his opinions are changing as the world and his perception of it changes. In 1975, while in America, he noted that he reads his past writings "like the text of a dead author."

Today, he considers Brecht's "theatre of enlightenment" an obsolete tool for the treatment of the complex reality of our age, and he is convinced that a new dramaturgy, a new concept of theatre, a new strategy of performance has to be created, or, rather different strategies for each prospective audience, as he himself demonstrated when he directed two productions of his play THE TASK, one at East Berlin's "Volksbühne" for that theatre's small studio stage, the second on the lavishly equipped main stage of the Bochum theatre in West Germany. The productions were drastically different, even though the same actor played the central part of Debuisson, since Müller knew he was addressing two utterly different audiences that brought to the performance vastly differing historical experiences. Müller regards theatre/performance as a means to influence audiences, and in this he still is in agreement with Brecht. It isn't the purpose of Brecht's theatre he is questioning, it is the method. Most of the plays regarded as belonging to Brecht's "mature," "classic" period, especially the parables, are, in Müller's opinion, not only outmoded but poor drama. What bothers him here is Brecht's attitude, the attitude of the man who knows better, who tries to manipulate one into accepting his answer as the only correct solution. Müller refuses to give answers; he offers the problem, poses the question, presents the conflicting attitudes and opinions, and challenges the spectator to take sides, or to withhold involvement. He doesn't pretend he knows more than his characters, he speaks "through their masks," as he wrote in our questionnaire, "I'M NEITHER A DOPE NOR A HOPE DEALER," published at the back of the volume; he is not the demiurge who creates his own controlled world on stage but a man who tries to rid himself of the contradictions life forces on him by giving them body and voice. In the *Semiotext(e)* interview he explained: "I believe in conflict. I don't believe in anything else. What I try to do in my writings is to strengthen the sense of conflicts, to strengthen confrontations and contradictions. There is no other way. I'm not interested in answers and solutions. I don't have any to offer. I'm interested in problems and conflicts."

Brecht, of course, also believed in putting contradictions on stage, but Müller sees in Brecht's later works an effort to escape these contradictions, to provide solutions and tutor the audience.

"Out of [Brecht's] revolutionary impatience with the immaturity of the conditions [for the revolution] stems the trend to substitute the proletariat, a trend that leads to paternalism, the disease of all Communist parties. In defense against the anarchic-natural matriarchy, the re-construction of the rebellious son into the father-figure begins, which makes for Brecht's success and hinders his impact. The relapse into popularity—by re-introduction of the Culinary that determined his later works—turned into an anticipation when the dementing maelstrom of the media sucked it up and Socialist cultural policy posthumously cemented the father-figure. What failed to take place was the present; his wisdom—a second exile. Brecht: an author without a present, a work between the past and the future. I hesitate to articulate this as a critique: the present is the age of the industrial nations: the history of the future won't be made by them, that's to be hoped; it will depend on their politics if we ought to fear the future. The categories 'wrong' or 'right' miss the essence of a work of art. Kafka's Statue of Liberty held a sword instead of a torch. It's treason to use Brecht without criticizing him."

Müller wrote this in 1980 in an essay *Fatzer ± Keuner*, whose title refers to the protagonist of Brecht's *Fatzer* fragment and the Keuner character of Brecht's collection of anecdotes, *Stories of Mr. Keuner*. Müller himself had two years earlier adapted a stage-version from the enormous fragment which Brecht never finished. He felt and still feels great affinity to the Brecht who struggled with the *Fatzer* epic, and who eventually admitted he couldn't resolve its problems and contradictions. Exactly in this aspect rests the greatness of *Fatzer* for Müller, namely that Brecht posed the conflicts but didn't force answers and easy solutions on the material.

It is this attitude that we can discover in THE TASK, in HAMLETMACHINE, and in QUARTET. As Müller explains in the questionnaire, he prefers drama to prose because: "Writing drama you always have masks you can talk through . . . I can say one thing and say the contrary." Of course, this ambiguity in the recent plays is disturbing to many of his critics, and they have attacked him for it. Müller seems rather to be amused by these attacks, and by the hype with which other critics praise his work, especially when his texts are taken literally, as direct reflections of political events or positions.

When the journalists of *Der Spiegel* volunteered such a literal interpretation of THE TASK, he replied: "You can't simply align politics and art on parallel tracks, I believe. If you translate an idea into an image, either the image will become askew or the idea will be exploded. I prefer the explosion."

His images that "explode ideas" have frequently been accused of being obscure and dense, even deliberately confusing not only Müller's audiences but his interpreters, too. In the *Spiegel* interview, he offers some advice to directors and actors: "My texts are frequently written so that every, or every second, sentence shows only the tip of the iceberg—and what's underneath is nobody's business. Then the theatre people put on their wetsuits and dive down, looking for the iceberg or building their own . . . That is hard to prevent, I have to live with it." On the confusion of his audience he remarked: "Isn't it a problem of the audience that refuses to accept that the theatre has a reality of its own and doesn't portray, mirror, or copy the reality of the audience? . . . Naturalism nearly killed the theatre with this strategy of doubling [reality]." Finally he commented on the "dark vision" his theatre supposedly presents of the world: "I find all my plays relatively funny. I never cease to be amazed that this comic aspect is noticed so rarely and used so little. I have written one true comedy, DIE UMSIEDLERIN. Maybe the fact that it was taken terribly seriously and that it resulted in my expulsion from the Writers Association is one reason why I've put on such a serious mask since." Again the reference to a mask Müller puts on. It is possible to see only the masks, and fail to recognize the man behind them, as the friend who, having read the plays in this edition, asked: Who *is* Heiner Müller?

******

Heiner Müller was born January 9, 1929, in Eppendorf, a small town in what used to be Saxony. Today the town belongs to the district of Karl Marx Stadt in the Southern part of the GDR. His family was of working class background, his father an office worker who had become a political activist and small functionary in the Social Democrat Party during the Weimar Republic after World War I. Müller was barely four years old when, on January 30, 1933, Hitler became Chancellor of the German Reich. Müller writes in his 1958 story "The Father": "January 31, 1933, at 4 a.m., my father, a functionary of the German Social Democrat Party, was arrested from his bed. I woke up, the sky outside the window black, noise of voices and footsteps. In the next room books were thrown onto the floor. I heard my father's voice, higher than the strangers' voices. I climbed out of my bed and went to the door. Through the crack of the door I watched as a man hit my father in the face. Shivering, the blanket up to my chin, I laid in bed when the door to my room opened. My father was standing in the doorway, behind him the strangers, big, in brown uniforms . . . I heard him call softly my name. I didn't answer and kept very quiet. Then my father said: He is asleep. The door was closed. I heard how they took him away . . ." Müller reflected on this event in the *Semiotext(e)* interview: "That is my guilt. I pretended I was sleeping. This really is the first scene of my theatre." This event, the experience of Fascist brutality and of his first "treason" in the face of it, became a trauma in Müller's life and work, as he has said on many occasions.

Indeed, the topos of treason appears in Müller's plays from the first to the last: The hero of DER LOHNDRÜCKER (THE SCAB) (1956), Balke, has committed treason—he informed on a Communist colleague in 1944 and caused the man's arrest; Jason in MEDEAMATERIAL betrays his barbarian wife. It is a topos, in Müller's case, inseparably linked to history, specifically German history from Hitler's terror to the present threat of nuclear holocaust. "One year after the arrest," he writes in "The Father," "my mother received permission to visit him in the camp . . . We stood in front of the wide gate with the wire mesh until they brought my father . . . The gate wasn't opened. He couldn't shake our hands

THE FARMERS, the revised version of *Die Umsiedlerin*,
at Volksbühne, East Berlin, 1976.

MACBETH, in Heiner Müller's own production at Volksbühne, East Berlin, 1982.

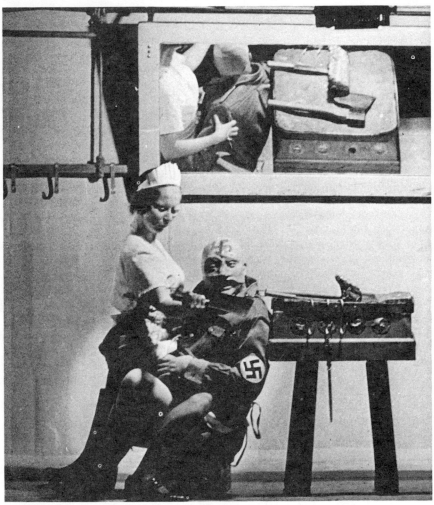

THE BATTLE, at Volksbühne, East Berlin, 1975.

through the fine mesh of the wire. I had to step close to the gate to see all of his thin face. He was very pale. I can't remember what was said. Behind my father, the armed guard stood, his face round and rosy." Müller explained to Lotringer: "I couldn't understand why he didn't jump over the fence."

More traumatic images: the well-fed face of those in power, the fence as a symbol of enforced separation. Another event of his childhood is recalled by Müller as "the second experience of treason": his father, eventually released from the concentration camp, wasn't able to find work. As a boy Müller had to write for an assignment in school an essay on the "Autobahn," the network of highways the Nazis built in the mid-thirties in Germany. His father first told him not to worry about it but then he proffered his help, advising Heiner to laud Hitler for building the Autobahn, and put into the essay a sentence stating his hope that "my father might get a job there." Müller mentioned later that this event estranged him from his father.

In the war years, Müller went to high school until he was drafted at the age of sixteen into the Labor Force (Reichsarbeitsdienst), during the final twitchings of the Hitler regime. In 1945, these young units were sent to the front, and he witnessed the last fighting in Mecklenburg in Northern Germany. Briefly a POW with the Americans, he managed after two days "to wander away quietly," as he put it. He simply began to walk home. "There were rumors that on entering the Soviet Zone all women were raped and the men slain. I expected to find the first corpses behind the shrubbery at the roadside. The Soviets gave us shelter and we got pea soup. The next morning we were assigned to a convoy that had to walk to the nearest county seat. There they gave us ten minutes to fade into the landscape and fend for ourselves. I made the hundred kilometers to my hometown in a few days." Müller described this final war experience to Jacques Poulet in an interview for *France Nouvelle*, January 29, 1979.

After the war, Müller eventually finished high school and worked for some time as a librarian. He began to write, so it seems, around this time.

* * * * * *

In 1949, the partition of Germany became final when the two German states, the Federal Republic of (West) Germany, and the (East) German Democratic Republic were constituted in short order. The "German schizophrenia," so decisive for Heiner Müller's writing, had become manifest.

His father who had again been a Social Democrat functionary after 1945 was expelled from the newly formed SED (Socialist Unity Party) into which Communists and Social Democrats had been fused. He was accused of being a "Titoist," because of "problems concerning the person of Stalin," Müller told Poulet. In 1951, his son met him after his defection in West Berlin. Müller described the encounter to Lotringer: "They discovered he had some kind of bacteria, something he never had before. So, he was put in a hospital and isolated. We talked through a glass door. He was standing on one side of the glass and I was standing on the other side. That was the next image." He refers to the glass door as another traumatic imprint in his memory, like the fence of the concentration camp and the door in which his arrested father stood. These images were to become important for his theatre.

When asked why he didn't consider following his father to the West, Müller replied: "I didn't really think about it then. Maybe I did identify with East Berlin or the Russian system more than he did. For the most part I wanted to be alone. I suppose it was a good way of getting rid of your parents . . . I believed in Communism. Stalin had nothing to do with it. I learned about Stalin through my father." His father eventually became a public servant in West Germany, administering pension payments to widows of Nazi officials and to former officers of the Wehrmacht, a fact Müller regarded as a paradox, an irony of history, but also as a kind of retribution. In his story "The Father" which he wrote six years after the defection, he accuses his father of trying "to keep himself out of the war of the classes," a theme which was going to become one of the central concerns of his later work.

The first major literary text of Müller was published by the cultural weekly *Sonntag* in a segment devoted to young authors, in December 1951. Titled "The People Are on The March," it was the story of a strike in a capitalist factory. The magazine introduced the piece as an "idiosyncratic treatment of the topic," but it didn't go against the grain of the ideological line all publications had to follow during those years of monolithic party rule in Stalin's realm. Throughout his early years as a writer, Müller's published texts don't show any disagreement with the aims and practice of the East German Republic and its controlling party, the SED.

June 17, 1953, a strike of construction workers at East Berlin's Stalinallee (Stalin Avenue) triggered a general uprising in the GDR that was spurred on by the Western media and squelched in three days by the Soviet army. The violent struggle left a deep and ambiguous impression on Müller. It wasn't until 1971, nearly twenty years later, however, that he dealt with the contradictions of those events in GERMANIA DEATH IN BERLIN. During the early fifties he had begun to sketch "counter scenes" to Brecht's *Private Life of the Master Race* (as the play is known in this country). Müller felt that Brecht had treated the phenomenon of "normal, everyday fascism" according to the yardstick of current Marxist theory, that consequently the true horror of the fascist mentality had eluded him. Müller's scenes were to correct this error. Yet, he didn't publish them until twenty years later; in the fifties, there wasn't much interest in an analysis of fascism that didn't fit the text-books. Through most of the decade, Müller made his living as a journalist, critic and editor for such magazines as *Sonntag* and *Junge Welt*, and he was briefly employed as a "scientific collaborator" with the "Schriftstellerverband," the Writers Association.

1956 was a crucial year for the further course of European history, and has become a kind of watershed in the history of Marxism. In February, Khrushchev revealed the full scope of Stalin's reign of terror during the XXth Soviet Party Congress. The debate on the abuses of the cult of Stalin began. Müller's mentor Brecht died in August. And in October, efforts to reform the Communist system in Hungary rapidly escalated into a full-scale revolution that was immediately exploited by the Cold War strategists and then crushed by invading Soviet forces after a week-long civil war. Many illusions on the left were shattered forever that year, many hopes brutally dashed. It was, of course, traumatic for Müller's development, as evident in his HAMLETMACHINE, a text he published twenty years later though the first scenes were written under the immediate impact of the events of '56. The following year his first play was published, DER LOHNDRÜCKER (the closest sense in English translation, though unsatisfactory, is THE SCAB). He had written it in collaboration with his wife Inge, and her experience as a factory worker was invaluable for this tale of conflicts among workers of a plant that, in 1948, had just become a "company owned by the people," and where the efforts of one foreman to introduce more efficient working methods encountered the violent resistance of his colleagues. The play belongs to a genre the party in the GDR encouraged in the fifties, the so-called "production play." The same year, 1957, the East Berlin radio commissioned a text from him; it became the first draft of THE CORRECTION. And at East Berlin's Volksbühne Müller received his first production, his play an adaptation of an American book, John Reed's *Ten Days That Shook The World*. Written in collaboration with the theatre's dramaturg, Hagen Müller-Stahl, it opened to positive reviews in November 1957.

Müller had become known in East Berlin by this time and was regarded as a most deserving, if provocative, talent. His stories and poems appeared in various magazines and literary journals, and in April 1958 Walter Ulbricht, the leader of the party and, in fact, if not in title, the ruler of the GDR, lauded publicly "the promising work of Heiner Müller." That same year the Maxim Gorki Theatre in East Berlin invited him to join its staff as "dramaturgic collaborator," a position Muller held until 1959.

******

It was in these years that I first met Heiner Müller. I was one of the young directors at the Berliner Ensemble where I had served since 1952 as an assistant to Brecht, as dramaturg and actor. Heiner asked if I would be interested in directing his play DER LOHNDRÜCKER. I wasn't only interested but flattered and quickly agreed. Müller arranged a meeting with the Artistic Director of the Gorki Theatre, Maxim Vallentin, to discuss the project. We had an amicable conversation and I explained my ideas for the production, yet Vallentin, one of the foremost representatives of "Socialist Realism," obviously wasn't impressed, or never intended to have an outsider from the Berliner Ensemble direct the play. In any case, I didn't hear from him again. Eventually, the play was premiered in Leipzig, and later opened at the Gorki Theatre, along with the revised version of THE CORRECTION, staged by a resident director of the company. When in 1959 Heiner and Inge Müller were awarded the prestigious Heinrich Mann Prize for DER LOHNDRÜCKER, it was the first widely visible recognition of their work.

******

During the mid-fifties, Müller had penned three poems, dedicated to the writers he seems to have admired and who most clearly influenced him. These free verses contain very concisely the view he held of the writer's lonesome place in history. They also reflect his perception of his own life during these troubled years.

BRECHT

Truly he lived in dark times.
The times have become brighter.
The times have become darker.
If brightness says, I am darkness
It spoke the truth.
If darkness says, I am
Brightness, it doesn't lie.

MAYAKOVSKY*

Mayakovsky, why
The leaden full stop?
Heartache, Vladimir?
"Has
A lady
Closed him out
Or
Opened
To someone else?"
Take
My bayonet
Out of your teeth
Comrades!
The walls stand
Speechless and cold
In the wind
The banners are clanking.

OR BÜCHNER, who died in Zürich
A hundred years before your birth
Age 23, for want of hope.

* * * * * *

It wasn't until 1961 that Müller completed another play, the year the Berlin Wall was erected and the partition of the city, and of Germany, cemented in concrete—a symbol for the divisions of our world, as Müller pointed out many years later. The new play was a comedy, DIE UMSIEDLERIN. The title is an untranslatable term that signifies a woman from the former Eastern provinces of the Reich, now being resettled in the GDR, as millions of Germans from those parts had to resettle in the two German states after World War II. The play was based on a story of the same title by Anna Seghers. The subtitle Müller gave his text states clearly its subject matter: DAS LEBEN AUF DEM LANDE (LIFE IN THE

---

* Heiner Müller recently completed an adaptation of Mayakovsky's first theatre text, *Vladimir Mayakovsky Tragedy*, which the poet wrote in 1913. Müller's version was staged September 9, 1983, at Berlin's Schiller Theater Werkstatt.

COUNTRY). Müller draws a large, yet detailed panorama of the conflicts and contradictions Socialist agricultural policy and its participants, supporters as well as enemies, had to struggle with. A student theatre production of the play in September 1961, barely seven weeks after the sealing of the GDR borders, was closed after one performance by the party authorities. Its content was obviously regarded as dangerously explosive or subversive. As a result of this event and the ensuing debates, Müller was expelled from the Writers Association. At the time, this was a very harsh and economically inauspicious punishment. For two years Müller was, more or less, an "undesirable person." He could not publish, nor were his plays produced anywhere. He told me once that only the support of some friends enabled him to survive as a writer; they commissioned radio plays—some were detective stories—which he wrote under assumed names.

In 1963, however, two longer poems were published in the literary journal *Forum*, and in 1964 he received, as member of a writers collective, the coveted Erich Weinert medal. A new play he had written, based on an acclaimed novel, *The Track of the Stones* by Erich Neutsch, was accepted for publication by the GDR's most respected literary journal, *Sinn und Form* (1/2, 1965). THE CONSTRUCTION SITE, once published, was soon attacked at the XIth Conference of the SED Central Committee in December 1965 for "Neglecting the dialectics of the [GDR's] development." Erich Honecker, presenting the report of the party's Polit Bureau, even quoted a line from Müller's play as proof of negative trends in the contemporary cultural scene: "Our reality is seen only as 'the ferry between the Ice Age and Communism,' " and, later in Honecker's report, the spade is called a spade: "If we want to increase productivity and with it our standard of living, we can't spread nihilistic, hopeless, and morally subversive philosophies in literature, film, theatre, television, and magazines." This sweeping indictment was aimed at Müller, Wolf Biermann, Stefan Heym, and other artists in the GDR. A scheduled production of THE CONSTRUCTION SITE in Leipzig was cancelled. Once again, Müller found himself in conflict with official doctrine and, consequently, isolated. He said later about this time that "even shaking my hand seemed to become a test of courage for many of my friends and colleagues in the GDR."

His wife Inge, who had a history of psychotic depression, committed suicide in 1966. Müller had been living for years with this threat, and once recorded in a poem the sorrows on his mind during one of his sleepless nights.

SELFPORTRAIT TWO AM
AUGUST 20, 1959

Sitting at the typewriter. Leafing
Through a detective story. Going to know
At the end what you already know
The smoothfaced aide with the ever growing stubble
Is the Senator's murderer
And the love of the young Sergeant from Homicide
For the Admiral's daughter will be returned.
But you won't be skipping one page.
Sometimes while turning the page a quick glance
At the blank sheet in the typewriter.

We will be spared at least that. That's something.
In the paper stood: somewhere a village
Has been razed to the ground by bombs.
It's regrettable, but does it concern you?
The Sergeant is just preventing the second murder
Though the Admiral's daughter (for the first time!)
Offers her lips, duty is duty.
You don't know how many are dead, the paper's gone.
Next door your wife dreams of her first love.
Yesterday she tried hanging herself. Tomorrow
She'll cut open her arteries or whatdoIknow.
At least she has a goal she can see
That she'll reach one way or another.
And the heart is a spacious graveyard.
The story of Fatima in Neues Deutschland*
Was so badly written that you had to laugh.
The torture is easier learned than describing the torture.
The killer has walked into the trap
The Sergeant embraces his prize.
Now you can sleep. Tomorrow's another day.

* * * * * *

Though there seemed little hope to see them produced, Müller finished two plays in 1966: HERAKLES 5 and PHILOCTETES, both based on Greek mythology, or drama, but giving the old stories surprising new turns. PHILOCTETES was to become the first of a trilogy that continued and expanded Brecht's model of the Lehrstück. However, Müller's more visible efforts during the next years were various translations or adaptations of classic and contemporary plays, among them a libretto based on Eugene Shvartz' play *The Dragon*, DRAGON OPERA, for the composer Paul Dessau, and written in collaboration with Ginka Cholakova who was to become Müller's second wife. His OEDIPUS TYRANT, after Sophokles, had a highly acclaimed production by Benno Besson at Deutsches Theater and in 1967 became the first of Müller's works to be produced in West Germany. When Hanns Lietzau staged the hugely successful premiere of PHILOCTETES at Munich's Residenz Theater the following year, Müller was recognized finally by West German critics as one of the leading playwrights in the language.

Müller finished the second play of the Lehrstück trilogy, THE HORATIAN (1968), which he based on the same Roman myth Brecht once used, though arriving at a very different conclusion; and in 1969 his adaptation of PROMETHEUS opened at the Zürich Schauspielhaus. When the next year he was invited to join the Berliner Ensemble, Brecht's former company, as a dramaturg, it was obvious that the tide had turned for Müller. Some people felt he might eventually assume Brecht's mantle as the "playwright-in-residence" of the Ensemble.

---

* Official daily newspaper of the SED. The war covered in the issue was the Algerian war of liberation from French rule.

With MAUSER, the last piece of his Lehrstück trilogy, he seemed to try a continuation in kind of Brecht's *The Measures Taken*. The densely constructed and highly poetic text presents only two characters, A and B, and a Chorus; it explores the question of revolutionary violence and results in the necessary acceptance of death by two Comrades to be executed for deeds committed in the service of the revolution. The play "looks into the white of history's eye," as Müller put it. He likes to quote a sentence by Ernst Jünger: "The blindness of an experience is the proof of its authenticity," pointing out that writing means to him "having an experience and, at the same time, formulating it in a way that others can share it." MAUSER marks a turning point in Müller's work. At issue is not so much the transmission of knowledge any more, but the task "to make experiences possible." The play has been attacked for its supposedly "Stalinist" position, a rather naive interpretation, totally misreading Müller's intentions. Yet, he never denied the fact that Stalin's reign was an integral part of Communism's history.

In 1971, he obviously felt he had enough distance from the disturbing events of the fifties to write about them in all their contradictions. He chose scenes sketched fifteen years earlier and extended them to a full-length play, GERMANIA DEATH IN BERLIN. The stretching of the Brechtian Epic model to its limits resulted here in the explosion of Brecht's "A-B-C dramaturgy," as Müller once referred to it. The text represents a sweeping panorama of German history, from the time of the Roman conquests to 1953, the year of the strikes and riots in the GDR. The events are shown partly in realistic scenes that employ poetically heightened language, partly in grotesquely exaggerated shapes that recall Grand Guignol, circus clowns, or the Bread and Puppet Theatre. The theme is the "German schizophrenia," the perennial war of brothers, from Arminius, tribal chief of the Cheruscans, whose brother Flavus fought him with the Roman legions, to the Nibelungs, Frederick II, and finally to a pair of brothers in Berlin, 1953, one a Communist, the other a former Nazi. A first example of the "synthetic fragment," the text consists of a rudimentary plot recounting events in the lives of various people from Berlin during 1953, yet disrupted by scenes from German myth and history which are presented in surreal, often grotesque, gory, or cartoon-like fashion; for instance, the Nibelungs appear at the battle of Stalingrad, Frederick II as a Clown or Vampire, Hitler and his consorts as the Holy Family, with a pregnant Goebbels giving birth to a Werewolf, etc. The play's wild, often violent, imagery and its terse, powerful language brings vividly to mind a line from a poem by Müller: "The terror I write about is of Germany."

The same year, 1971, Erich Honecker, newly installed chief of the SED, proclaimed at the VIIIth Party Congress: "There should be no taboos anymore for the arts as long as [the artist] stands on a firm Socialist position." The climate had changed. That year, Müller wrote his version of MACBETH, as unrelenting a reading of a Shakespearean fable as Edward Bond's *Lear*. It was soon produced at Brandenburg, near Berlin, quickly followed by productions in West Germany and Switzerland. MACBETH provoked a massive attack in *Sinn und Form* (1, 1973), by the prominent critic Wolfgang Harich, once a victim of Ulbricht who had him imprisoned in 1956. Harich's essay started the discussion about Müller's so-called "historical pessimism," a debate picked up later with a vengeance by some West German critics, as, for instance, Michael Schneider in *Literatur Konkret*, Fall

1979. While THE HORATIAN was produced at West Berlin's Schiller Theatre in 1973, Müller finished a play for the Berliner Ensemble. CEMENT was based on a Russian novel of the same title, written in the twenties by Fjodor Gladkov. It opened that same year, directed by Ruth Berghaus, with music by Paul Dessau. The play had a man-woman relationship at its center, going much further in this respect than, for instance, the earlier CONSTRUCTION SITE, and showing the conflicts of a married couple during the turmoils and struggles of the Russian civil war. Experimenting further in his "synthetic fragment" mode, Müller inserted material based on the Prometheus and Hercules myths.

The "montage" of various scenes he had written in the fifties and sixties was completed and became the texts TRAKTOR and THE BATTLE (1974), while at the same time his plays were being produced by the most prestigious companies in East and West Berlin, and in increasing number in West Germany, during the following years. There was also the first staging of a Müller play in a Socialist country outside the GDR, CEMENT, at Hungary's National Theatre, Budapest, in 1975. Official recognition was not lacking either: twice in the seventies he received the Prize of the East Berlin theatre critics, and, in 1975, one of the most important literary awards of the GDR, the Lessing Prize.

The same year Müller was invited to the University of Texas at Austin as a writer in-residence. When Ruth Berghaus was forced to resign as the Artistic Director of the Berliner Ensemble, Müller also left the company, and in the Fall of 1975 he arrived at Austin. While in Austin, he collaborated on the first staging of his last Lehrstück, MAUSER, when it was produced by a student company. The all-women cast presented the piece as an aggressively feminist statement, an interpretation with which Müller was quite pleased, as he was, during his second visit to the U.S. (1979) with the Berkeley Stage Company production of CEMENT. After a semester in Austin, he and his wife travelled widely throughout the States and in Mexico. What he saw and what he heard left a deep and permanent impression on his thinking and his writing. Here, in America, he wrote his PROJECTION 1975:

Where is the morning we saw yesterday

The early bird is singing through the night
In his red coat morning is walking through
The dew that glistens from its steps like blood

I'm reading what I've written three, five, twenty years ago like the text of a dead author, from an age when a death still could be fitted into verse. The killers ceased to scan their victims. I remember my first effort to write a play. The script got lost in the confusion of the post-war years. It began with the—youthful—hero standing in front of a mirror trying to discover which road the maggots would take through his flesh. At the end he stood in the basement and cut open his father. In the century of Orestes and Electra that's rising Oedipus will be a comedy.

* * * * * *

After Müller returned to Berlin, he accepted a position as dramaturg with East Berlin's Volksbühne. Some of his earlier but only one of the recent plays had their premieres at this theatre: THE FARMERS, a revised version of DIE UM-

SIEDLERIN, in 1976; THE CONSTRUCTION SITE and THE TASK in 1980. Here, he also began to direct his texts, first THE TASK—he directed another production two years later in Bochum, West Germany—and then MACBETH, in the Fall of 1982, the spectacular production invited but not performed at the Holland Festival the following year.

In recent years, his plays have been produced all over Europe in increasing numbers. There have been more than 25 productions in the GDR by now, nearly 100 in West Germany, 15 in Austria, more than 12 in Switzerland, and in translations his plays have been performed in England, Holland, France, Belgium, the U.S., Scandinavia, Italy, Poland, Hungary, Bulgaria, Yugoslavia, Iraq, and one production is even documented for South Africa. In 1979, at the Mülheim Festival for New Drama, Müller was awarded the most prestigious West German Prize for playwrights, the Mülheimer Dramatikerpreis, for his GERMANIA DEATH IN BERLIN.

******

As he explains in the questionnaire, Heiner Müller holds a rather dim view of success. He'd rather "split," unsettle, provoke his audience. Writing about the dance theatre of Pina Bausch, he pointed out that in her theatre "the image is a thorn in our eye." That is exactly what Heiner Müller is trying to achieve in his own theatre: to pierce our eye so we'll be able to see better. He wants us to recognize that "The first shape of hope is fear, the first appearance of the new: Horror" as he said on several occasions. And he insists that he, as a person, should be of no interest: "My main existence is in writing. The other level of existence is just perfunctory." In a poem which became part of his text "The Father," he once stated:

I'd wish my father was a shark
Who tore to pieces forty whalers
(And in their blood I'd learned to swim)
My mother a blue whale my name Lautréamont
Died in Paris 1871 unknown

1871 was, of course, the year of the Paris Commune.

Carl Weber
New York

The Correction

THE CORRECTION (*Die Korrektur*) was conceived as a radio play in 1957. It was published in *Neue Deutsche Literatur*, Nr. 5, 1958, Berlin. After a presentation of the play to members of the combine "Black Pump," the text elicited a favorable response from the workers, engineers and administrators, though some criticized it for its neglect "of the positive aspects" and "of the workers' struggle to fulfill our plan." A preview of the first stage version, however, caused massive criticism of the "depressive" effects of the play. Müller replied to these complaints in a statement: "The author's self-critique has entered an executive phase: *The Correction* will be corrected. The new literature can only be developed together with our new audience" (*Neue Deutsche Literatur*, Nr. 1, 1959), and he went on to analyze the shortcomings of the play.

A revised version had its first performance, together with DER LOHNDRÜCKER, in a staging by H. D. Maede on September 2, 1958, at the Maxim Gorki Theatre in Berlin. In the second version a prologue is added, introducing in doggerel rhymes the characters of the play. The story and the conflicts of Bremer, the protagonist, are less prominent; the monologues of various characters are reduced in size and number; some controversial statements have been eliminated; the positive function of the party is emphasized; the play ends with an uplifting monologue spoken by the young Heinz B. who joined the party in the last scene. In general, the dramaturgy seems to follow a more conventional pattern.

When I discussed the selection of plays for this volume, Heiner Müller insisted on the original version of the radio play.

A footnote: While working on THE CORRECTION in 1957, Müller told me he was writing a play he'd like to call "Death of a Foreman"—this seems to indicate that he once was thinking of a tragic ending.

C.W.

33

A report on the building of the industrial combine "Black Pump."*

A FOREMAN

BREMER Are you the secretary?

PARTY SECRETARY Yes. What is it?

BREMER My name is Bremer, I've been in the party since 1918, was in a concentration camp until '45, functionary until a week ago. The party ordered me to go into the field because I hit a Nazi in the face, he had a position with the National Front. And now I am here at the combine.

PARTY SECRETARY Good, Comrade Bremer. You'll work in section 6 as foreman. *Pause.* You're going to have problems. Socialism isn't built with socialists only, not here and not elsewhere, and here least of all. The combine is a construction site, not a model plant, and we have to build fast. Our industry needs electricity and coal, and it needs both fast. You won't make it if you don't stick with the party.

BREMER You are the party here, right?

PARTY SECRETARY The party has placed me here. You can criticize me when I make mistakes. That's what meetings are for. For that too.

STORY OF THE WORKER FRANZ K.

FRANZ K. I am a construction worker, red since 1918, not as red anymore since '46. I've turned the Erzgebirge mountains upside down for Wismut†. Eight hours a day, in uninspected pits that could flood any day. Whoever didn't drown in the pit drowned in vodka. Whoever wasn't wiped out by the vodka was finished off by the

---

*Huge industrial complex for the mining and processing of lignite, built in the '50s.
†Soviet-owned company for the mining of uranium ore.

women. It was hard to stay clear of it: of the pits, of the women, of the vodka. Now, things have improved: the pits are inspected and the women are married. I didn't break my back here at the combine. If management thinks it's going too slow why doesn't management visit us at the building site? Sometimes they send a dispatcher on a motorcycle. He arrives in a cloud of dust, makes a lot of noise, and disappears again in a cloud of dust before we can get a word in edgeways. But in the meetings they address us as "the working class." At least they could make sure that we have no waiting periods. We're waiting for the blue prints. We're waiting for material. That pushes down wages. We know what we're worth and do nothing without pay. Before we let them cheat us, we take care of our own ass first: wages rise faster than the walls, the wage curve faster than production. The foremen write the time sheets the way we need them and the supervisor closes both his eyes. It isn't his loss. Bremer was the first who didn't play ball. He kept repeating: That's fraud. Fraud is out of the question. He didn't play ball, not for the beatings he got, and not for the beer we offered him. He is red to the marrow.

THE SWING OF NORMS

THE "MAJOR" Get on the swing, foreman. On the swing of norms.

FRANZ K. He is new. He knows from nothing. Show him the light, Major.

MAJOR Now listen, foreman. You're new here and know from nothing. Here, this is the norm, established by one pushy bastard with six assistants, he got a bonus for it: a blatant injustice. It has to be adjusted. Corrected. What we don't make on the job we'll make on paper. The pencil is yours. You need only to compute, that's all.

HEINZ B. That's the swing of norms. *Laughter.*

FRANZ K. The waiting periods push the wages down, we're pushing back. And the norm remains where it is.

FOREMAN Fraud is out of the question.

MAJOR I wouldn't call it fraud.

FOREMAN What sort of a guy are you? Why do you call him major?

FRANZ K. He was a captain. We promoted him to major. He is a rat. But he is right about the norm.

FOREMAN Actually, what are you working for?

HEINZ B. For money. *Laughter.*

FOREMAN I know what I am working for.

FRANZ K. So? You know that? *Sings:* The Pole gets the coal, the Czech gets the light . . . *Continues talking:* For that, right?

MAJOR Write two hundred percent. We won't do it for less. We have our fixed price.

FOREMAN On my sheet is written: hundred and twenty. Hundred and twenty is what we've done.

FRANZ K. Right. And that's not enough. Therefore, we round it off and write two hundred.

FOREMAN If you want to earn more, work more.

MAJOR A proposal, foreman. One case of beer for an arithmetical error. Premium beer.

FOREMAN I'll get you to Waldheim,* you rat.

MAJOR What do you mean, Waldheim? We're deaf on that ear. But we do need the two hundred. If the beer won't do it, we'll talk plain language. Whoever isn't with us is against us.

FOREMAN Fraud is out of the question. As long as I am foreman here.

MAJOR Then go and apply for another position right away.

STORY OF THE ENGINEER MARTIN E.

MARTIN E. The combine is a construction site. When it's completed, the largest lignite-combine in the world will be completed. Then we won't lack anymore the bituminous coal the Ruhr barons are sitting on. Whatever can be made from lignite we will make here: in briquet factories, power plants and carbonization plants. In the meantime, we're building, with new methods and with old ones. Here, a man sits at an instrument panel and controls a machine that replaces a hundred workers. Within a stone's throw, three men, sweating and badly paid, dig a trench with tools like the old Romans used. Many a plant is administered by the method: My friend, the plan. That looks like this: The plant is in debt so we rename the plant; gone it is and so are the debts. After all, the plant is owned by the people, after all, it belongs to nobody, you can do with it as you please, the state will foot the bill. There are other stories the newspapers won't print. The one about the union functionary in the women's dorm won't be printed either. That was in the early days: he had been assigned to watch so nothing happened to the women. Every night the colleagues climbed through the windows and that didn't help their

---

*Well known penitentiary.

job performance. Yet, he couldn't stay up all night. So he laid down to sleep among the women. When the secretary appointed another man to watch the watchman, he slept there too. That's class consciousness for you. Or the story of working in the forest with the girls from the Spremberg spinning mill. We had female help from a spinning mill to clear the site and, since it was mid-summer, we called the HO* to deliver soda. The HO shipped us wine. The wine was swilled like soda. The girls were chased through the woods. The trees were not cut down. Those were the wild days. The forest is cleared now, the site is leveled. The first buildings are up: smokestacks, cooling towers, the steel frame of the assembly shops, foundations, and the satellite town for the workers is going up in Hoyerswarda. The landscape doesn't look like itself anymore. To rebuild man takes more time. I know what's going on in the bars at night: The "gold diggers" who are always on the move hang out there. They always follow their nose. They smell money from a hundred miles. They "subscribe" to big building sites. Hardships only make them smirk. They earn a lot and drink even more, they go home and cuss as they pass the posters proclaiming Socialism, and in the morning they are at their job and build Socialism with a hangover. During meetings they abuse the front office engineers. The engineers listen. To rebuild man takes time.

REGULATIONS

ENGINEER C. *On the telephone.* Construction office, engineer C, Section 6, please, building management.—Listen, you've got to suspend work on the foundations immediately.—Until further notice.—Three days, two weeks, what do I know.—Pay attention, I'll tell you precisely what's happened. We received the blueprints for the bunker from Central planning, as usual. There's been a mistake in one of the drawings.—No, nothing complicated, as far as we could determine. Easy to correct. But we can't do anything without talking to Berlin.—The blueprint has to go back, to be checked, discussed and redrawn. We have to wait.—That's normal.—You must deal with the workers.—Those guys have to wait too.—The plan? The plan has to wait too.—Won't work? How do you know what's going to work. *Puts the receiver down.*

ENGINEER E. That won't do.

ENGINEER C. What do you mean?

ENGINEER E. I say it won't do. The plan cannot wait.

ENGINEER C. *Thinks it over.* All right. Tell the project director the blueprints will be with the brigades by tomorrow at noon. We'll get them ready.

ENGINEER E. It's against regulations.

ENGINEER C. Yes. We have to take the risk.

---

*Handels Organisation: State-owned Trade organization.

ENGINEER E. We won't be ready by noon.

ENGINEER C. We still have the night. Tomorrow at noon the blueprints will be with the brigades.

ENGINEER R. *At the telephone.* Construction office. Please, section 6, building management.

STORY OF THE WORKER HEINZ B.

HEINZ B. My father croaked in the coal pits of the Ruhr. My mother froze to death at the Ruhr, in the winter of '47, because I was in jail for stealing coal and couldn't filch coal anymore. Later I met a girl from East Germany. She told me there were jobs and so I went. We planned to marry, that takes money. That's how we came to the combine. She was a mechanic. She made a good salary, more than I did, and she got bonuses for excellent work. After three months I noticed she was doing overtime at night too. Two bricklayers were beating each other up on the site. That's when it came out. One of them had offered her twelve Marks. He was a foreman, and she had told him: Fritz isn't a foreman and is paying thirteen; I won't let a foreman have it for less than fifteen. I asked her: What do I owe you, and can I pay it in installments, I won't be able to make it in one trip, what with her scale. Now she is where I came from, in the West. She can't score there as a mechanic, as a whore yes. We had already picked an apartment, with bath and incinerator, at Hoyerswerda in those new developments. The building was ready, they had only forgotten the sewers. Else we would have moved in and I'd have thrown her down the incinerator chute. Shortly after, I quit at the VEB* because our foreman was an asshole. I said that too loudly and management got me by the tail. I got a job with a private firm. The workers were married to the company. I had sworn to myself I'd never marry. But the work clicked along: they didn't waste materials, the deadlines were kept. I asked myself: Why can't it be like that at the VEB? The boss said: We are one big family. That meant: overtime and no pay. I wasn't used to that. As he pats my back and says: I won't ask you what party you belong to, I ask him: Which one do you prefer, boss? He took that amiss. I left because of the overtime, back to the VEB. The new foreman was an eager beaver. The ditty "The foreman's pencil likes to hear / the clinking of a case of beer" didn't apply to him. We beat him up since we thought maybe he'd listen to that tune. He didn't hit back. He got up and wiped the blood off. He didn't play ball for anything. He said: Fraud is out of the question. If you want to earn more, work more. Then, the major set him up in the tavern. He took Franz K.'s slide rule away and planted it in the foreman's pocket. It was supposed to look as if he had stolen it. A slide rule comes to about two Marks, but the colleagues believed it, K. first of all. That really shook the foreman. Then the scandal with the foundation happened. It crumbled because we didn't remix the concrete. You know what the problem is with the concrete: We get it from the mixing tower. That runs automatically and is the hottest new thing around. But management lent special trucks for transporting the concrete to another plant when we had a waiting period. We haven't seen them again. So, the concrete dries

---

*Volks Eigener Betrieb: People-Owned Enterprise.

up during transport and we have to remix it. That takes time and our money. I said: It's too dry. It'll settle all right, said the major. The foreman doesn't let us earn what we need. We've got to look after our own ass. Time is money. Franz K. said: We already had to wait for the blueprints, and it's not the first time. Shall we lose money because the intelligentsia is late? Are we sitting on featherbeds? It doesn't have to go wrong, he said. That business about the blueprints is correct. Normally it's like this: everything is built in one piece, but only when the project is completely designed. The combine is delivered by the slice: One slice designing, one slice building. But we didn't remix the concrete. The foreman wasn't present. He controlled the casings in the adjoining section. After it happened he asked: What have you done? The major said: The same as usual. The foreman was responsible for our work. He got stuck with it.

FOUNDATIONS

THE CHAIRMAN The corner foundation of site 6 is crumbling. It has to be ripped out and poured over. Bremer's brigade was working there. They did poor work. It has to be investigated.

A FEMALE WORKER We demand that the accident on the railway tracks be investigated. A lines woman was run over at the intersection of tracks and mainroad. The truck didn't stop when she gave the block signal, she had to jump aside onto the track and the train engine ran her over. She has four children and she's in the hospital now, both legs gone, she's dying because the truck driver was in a hurry.

A YOUNG WORKER He's paid by the number of runs.

THE WOMAN He kills by the number.

THE YOUNG WORKER He sounded his horn.

THE WOMAN He didn't stop.

A HOARSE MAN If we always wait for you womenfolk we'll never manage.

THE WOMAN I know you. We're the fifth wheel when your pennies are at stake. When you want to hump us you'll pay any price.

THE HOARSE MAN I won't make you a child anymore, Prohaska.

THE WOMAN I can make my children myself. I don't need you for it, you old goat. We demand that the accident be investigated.

FIRST WORKER First the foundation.

THE WOMAN We demand a hearing. We work like you do. That's a foundation too.

CHAIRMAN We don't deny that. Your demand is justified, the accident will be investigated, the truck driver punished if it's clear that he is guilty. But one thing at a time, the most important first. You've got to understand that.

THE WOMAN We're not important, are we? Why don't you pour us into your foundation with the concrete?

CHAIRMAN Because we don't build this combine for the heck of it. We can't help the injured colleague if the doctors can't help her. We'll help her children if we build better and faster. So, first the foundation.

SECOND WORKER Where are the children?

THE WOMAN In the maternity home.

SECOND WORKER Does she have a family?

THE WOMAN No.

SECOND WORKER So we've got to see what happens to the children now.

THIRD WORKER We have another complaint here. A Sorbian* farmer complains that a truck carrying lumber took a shortcut across his beet field.

CHAIRMAN Call him in. But he ought to make it brief.

A farmer enters.

A FARMER A truck from the combine drove across my beet field. I want damages. I have already lost three fields to your combine. The Russians gave them to me. You want them for your Socialism now, and your Socialism is driving trucks across my only beet field.

FIRST WORKER Our Socialism listens to the name of Fritz Erpen. We've warned him twice before. His last job was with a circus. Fire eater. He's drinking his gas away. Then, he hasn't enough of it and needs to take short cuts.

CHAIRMAN Is he here?

THE WORKER No.

THE FARMER I want damages.

THE HOARSE MAN Don't steal our time. We've got more to do than to listen to your wailing, Polack.

---

*A Slavic minority in the Southeast of the GDR.

THE FARMER I am a Sorbian.

THE HOARSE MAN That's the same.

THE FARMER Polack is what the SS used to call me. Now the word is Sorbian.

THE HOARSE MAN Two of your people are working with us at the bunker, Sorbian. Who will pay us damages if they push up the norm for us because they want to butter up management? I know what's going on.

CHAIRMAN We'd be ahead if you'd work half as much as our Sorbian colleagues.

THE FARMER I'll be short of beets. I didn't determine the debit.

CHAIRMAN Get your damages from the main office. Whoever drives through your field will be fired. Anything else?

THE FARMER I'll ram the pitchfork into his tires the next time. *Exits.*

CHAIRMAN Now the foundation, Bremer, you are the foreman. You've poured the foundation. What do you have to say?

BREMER We worked as usual. There must be a mistake in the drawing. That's what happens if the eggheads don't show their faces on the site. If something goes wrong when they are careless, they blame the workers.

ENGINEER I am the engineer responsible. I did the drawing. It is correct. You bet your life. It has been double-checked. I am not responsible for the execution. Who are you anyway? You are new here, aren't you?

BREMER I did eight years in a concentration camp. You filled your bellies during those years and designed war planes for Hitler, as armament specialists. You've ruined everything and made a healthy bundle doing it. And now you're profiting from it. We have to rebuild what you destroyed.

CHAIRMAN Enough, Comrade Bremer. Stick to the facts: The foundation. The engineer is right. The drawing is correct. You are responsible for the execution.

BREMER I don't trust anyone who worked for Hitler. And that's a fact.

ENGINEER That is a defamation. Cooperation is impossible on this basis. I demand that this man be fired. *Leaving.* I won't put up with this.

VOICE That's the last we saw of him.

CHAIRMAN Comrade Bremer, you will apologize to the engineer. He can't leap out of his skin. He is giving us everything he has in his head. You have no right to insult him.

BREMER I'd tear myself to pieces for Socialism. But I won't crawl into an engineer's behind.

CHAIRMAN Not even for Socialism? Think about it, fast. What is the matter with the foundation? *Pause. Agitation.*

HEINZ B. Foreman, we didn't remix the concrete. That could have been it. The concrete dried up during transport because we've got no special trucks. We wanted to save time.

FRANZ K. We already had to wait for the drawing.

CHAIRMAN I see: Three weeks time was lost because you fought for the minute. Not to mention the expenses. Bremer, what do you say now? You blame the engineer that he is costing money and doesn't care for the brigades. Your brigade committed sabotage and you were in charge. The foundation costs more than an engineer.

BREMER That's no brigade, that's a bunch of bums.

VOICE You're a good foreman, only the brigade is good for nothing, right?

BREMER In the concentration camp I knew why I was doing time. Now I know nothing anymore.

STORY OF THE PARTY SECRETARY

PARTY SECRETARY I came back to Germany from the Soviet Union late in '44, parachute dropped into Pomerania on a party assignment. What I saw was worse than we had expected. Lower middle class women decked out with their husbands' conquests: dresses from Paris, furs from the East. Mothers who pushed their children into the army. Widows in proud mourning. And our comrades on death row. At that time I thought: we ought to hack off each hand that stirred for Hitler. Today I see how this combine is built, with such hands too. I read the transcript of the production meeting in which Bremer insulted an engineer. The engineer threatened to quit. Bremer refused to apologize. All his life he put his head on the line for the party but he couldn't get this into his head. I had to summon him. It wasn't easy for me. I could understand that he didn't understand what the party asked of him.

THE CORRECTION

PARTY SECRETARY Bremer, the engineer is threatening to quit. We have to settle this mess. You've blamed him without justification. So, you have to apologize to him. I understand it's hard on you but it has to be done.

BREMER So that's where we are now. I am wrong. Maybe the engineer did time in the concentration camp for the party, and I designed war planes for Hitler?

PARTY SECRETARY You did time in the concentration camp for the party, the engineer designed war planes for Hitler. No one is questioning that. But we are building the combine. We need the engineer. You've failed as foreman, you have offended him without reason, and the party demands that you settle this mess.

BREMER So that's where we are now.

PARTY SECRETARY We can afford to build Socialism even with people who are not interested in Socialism. That's where we are now. We cannot do without them. We are not there yet. And when we get there it won't be necessary anymore because they will be interested in Socialism.

BREMER Do you still know where is right and where is left? I fought on the barricades in 1918, on the right side: on the left. I still know where the enemy is.

PARTY SECRETARY We don't need any barricades, Comrade Bremer, we need industrial combines. We have to work Capitalism against the wall. If you don't understand that you have understood nothing. We demand that you apologize.

BREMER I won't make a fool of myself. The eggheads are laughing at us.

PARTY SECRETARY They are working for us.

BREMER They're paid for it, and more than enough.

PARTY SECRETARY There aren't enough of them yet.

BREMER So the party demands that I crawl on my belly before a bourgeois engineer.

PARTY SECRETARY To correct your mistake.

STORY OF THE ENGINEER HERBERT C.

ENGINEER C. It never happened to me before that a worker dared to challenge me like that. I always delivered clean work, correct even under trying circumstances like these. What happens on the building site is not my concern. I am an engineer. Two days after the production meeting about the botched foundation in section 6, I led a delegation through the building grounds—students, journalists, technical experts form Czechoslovakia. Bremer approached me near the cooling towers. He had a slip of paper in his hand. He looked tired. I nearly felt pity for him. He handed me the slip and walked on. He'd written on the paper: I take back the accusation I've made against engineer C. during the production meeting. It doesn't correspond to the facts. Bremer. One of the journalists asked me about the relation between workers and intellectuals at the combine. Good, I said.

THE AGREEMENT

HEINZ B. I want to join the party, foreman.

BREMER I'm not a foreman anymore.

HEINZ B. But you're in the party. I smashed the major's nasal bone. Will that be favorably considered for my application period?

BREMER It isn't our task to smash nasal bones. We are the ruling class. Our weapon is the state. You want to join the party. Do you know what you're bargaining for? A lot will be asked of you. Less beer, more work. Up to the navel in mud if need be. Getting up when you've fallen and getting up again when you've fallen again. And don't believe there will be a position in the bargain. The party is no social service. How many women do you have? Count carefully. Two are too many.

HEINZ B. None.

BREMER That may be too few. But you've got time. So: You know what you're doing?

HEINZ B. Yes.

BREMER Good. Then talk to the secretary. And what'll happen with the foundation?

HEINZ B. We'll do the foundation over.

BREMER I'll break your skull if it crumbles again. Agreed?

HEINZ B. Agreed.

END

Medeaplay

MEDEAPLAY (*Medeaspiel*) was written in 1974. It was published in *Heiner Müller: Texte 3, Rotbuch 134*, Berlin 1975, as his first scenario, without any specified text to be spoken. No production of the play is on record.

The piece is Müller's first published exploration of a theatre of images. Its theme was picked up again in MEDEAMATERIAL, the centerpiece of his last text.

C.W.

47

A bed is lowered from the flies and put upright on stage. Two female figures with death masks lead a girl on stage and place her with her back to the bed. Dressing of the bride. She is tied to the bed with the belt of her wedding dress. Two male figures with death masks lead the bridegroom in and place him facing the bride. He stands on his head, walks on his hands, turns cartwheels before her, etc.; she laughs without a sound. He rips up the wedding dress and takes his place with the bride. Projection: The Sexual Act. The male death masks tie the hands of the bride to the bed with the shreds of the wedding dress, and the female death masks her feet. The remains serve to gag her. While the man stands on his head, walks on his hands, turns cartwheels, etc. before the (female) spectators, the woman's belly swells until it bursts. Projection: The Act of Birth. The female death masks pull a child from the woman's belly, untie her hands, place the child in her arms. Meanwhile, the male death masks have draped the man with so many arms that he can move only on all fours. Projection: The Act of Killing. The woman takes off her face, rips up the child, and hurls the parts in the direction of the man. Debris, limbs, intestines fall from the flies on the man.

END

Hamletmachine

HAMLETMACHINE (*Hamletmaschine*) was completed in 1977 and published in *Theater Heute*, Nr. 12, Seelze 1977. The world premiere was staged by Jean Jourdheuil on January 30, 1979, together with a production of MAUSER, at the Théâtre Gérard Philipe in Saint Denis, near Paris. (An earlier effort to produce the play in Cologne was given up after two weeks of rehearsal; this experiment is documented in: Theo Girshausen, *Müllers Endspiel*, Prometh Verlag, Köln 1978.)

According to the author, he was attracted to the Hamlet story since he first labored through the original in 1946, with the aid of a dictionary. In his opinion, Hamlet is "much more a German than an English character . . . the intellectual in conflict with history." Since the early fifties, Müller believes, the character has again become topical as in Brecht's perspective of the Danish prince: the man between the ages.

Müller wrote the first scenes for a Hamlet play in the fifties. The text published here was quickly written after Müller had translated *Hamlet* for a production by Benno Besson at the Volksbühne in East Berlin. The 200-page play he had conceived shrunk to eight pages, "the shrunken head of the Hamlet tragedy," as he likes to call it. He tried to create a variant of the Hamlet theme in a Communist country after Stalin's death, the story of the son of a high party functionary whose father died under obscure circumstances, yet later received a state funeral; i.e., Hamlet in the Hungary of 1956, a story reminiscent of the Rajk affair.

In a conversation about the text in 1979, Müller said that while he was writing the play "there was no historical substance for real dialogues, it turned into separate monologues of Hamlet and Ophelia. It became, more than ever anticipated, a self-critique of the intellectual. . . . It is the description of a petrified hope, an effort to articulate a despair so it can be left behind. It certainly is a 'terminal point,' I can't continue in this way." He added that for him "there is a cycle starting with DER LOHNDRÜCKER and concluded by HAMLETMACHINE." It is indeed his last play that deals in a direct way with Communist history of the twentieth century

Müller stated about the other protagonist: "Ophelia has to do with Ulrike Meinhoff and the problem of terrorism in Europe, a complex issue that was very much, and in a very ambivalent way, on my mind while I wrote the piece. . . . The Ophelia-character is a criticism of Hamlet, consequently a self-critique; it contains autobiographical material dealing with the man-woman relationship of today." In an American production, Müller felt "the main character here could rather be Ophelia than Hamlet. I wouldn't consider this as a disadvantage . . . it was my intention to make Ophelia a character of equal importance. That could become an interesting aspect in the U.S."

The last sentence of Ophelia's text, "When she walks . . ." quotes Squeaky Fromme who tried to assassinate President Ford. Müller explained, "I found it interesting that the Manson family was the pragmatic, unideological, puritan, Christian variant of European terrorism in the U.S.A. And I mean 'puritan' as of the origins, only a puritan-oriented society can produce such extremes. I believe the sentence contains a truth which wasn't necessarily known to that girl." Of course, the text contains numerous other quotes and allusions. It is probably Müller's most complicated text, and the most difficult to decode. "The title, HAMLET-MACHINE," Müller said in a *Theater Heute* interview, April 1982, "was an accident. There was a project to print all of my texts that had to do with Shakespeare. We racked our brains for a title and hit upon 'Shakespeare's Factory' since I found that quite smart. And there was this play I had no title for and since I wanted an illustration from a book by Duchamp for the edition, the title HAMLETMACHINE resulted automatically. That was eventually interpreted: Hamletmachine = H.M. = Heiner Müller. I carefully disseminated this interpretation."

C.W.

52

Claude Le-Anh

HAMLETMACHINE, at Théâtre Gérard Philipe in Saint-Denis, 1979.

1

FAMILY SCRAPBOOK

I was Hamlet. I stood at the shore and talked with the surf BLABLA, the ruins of
Europe in back of me. The bells tolled the state-funeral, murderer and widow a
couple, the councillors goose-stepping behind the highranking carcass' coffin,
bawling with badly paid grief WHO IS THE CORPSE IN THE HEARSE/ABOUT
WHOM THERE'S SUCH A HUE AND CRY/'TIS THE CORPSE OF A GREAT/
GIVER OF ALMS the lane formed by the populace, creation of his statecraft HE
WAS A MAN HE TOOK THEM ALL FOR ALL. I stopped the funeral procession,
I pried open the coffin with my sword, the blade broke, yet with the blunt
reminder I succeeded, and I dispensed my dead procreator FLESH LIKES TO
KEEP THE COMPANY OF FLESH among the bums around me. The mourning
turned into rejoicing, the rejoicing into lipsmacking, on top of the empty coffin the
murderer humped the widow LET ME HELP YOU UP, UNCLE, OPEN YOUR
LEGS, MAMA. I laid down on the ground and listened to the world doing its turns
in step with the putrefaction.
I'M GOOD HAMLET GI'ME A CAUSE FOR GRIEF*
AH THE WHOLE GLOBE FOR A REAL SORROW*
RICHARD THE THIRD I THE PRINCE-KILLING KING*
OH MY PEOPLE WHAT HAVE I DONE UNTO THEE*
I'M LUGGING MY OVERWEIGHT BRAIN LIKE A HUNCHBACK
CLOWN NUMBER TWO IN THE SPRING OF COMMUNISM
SOMETHING IS ROTTEN IN THIS AGE OF HOPE*
LET'S DELVE IN EARTH AND BLOW HER AT THE MOON*
Here comes the ghost who made me, the ax still in his skull. Keep your hat on, I
know you've got one hole too many. I would my mother had one less when you
were still of flesh: I would have been spared myself. Women should be sewed
up—a world without mothers. We could butcher each other in peace and quiet,
and with some confidence, if life gets too long for us or our throats too tight for our

---

*The lines with an asterisk are in English in the German text.

screams. What do you want of me? Is one state-funeral not enough for you? You old sponger. Is there no blood on your shoes? What's your corpse to me? Be glad the handle is sticking out, maybe you'll go to heaven. What are you waiting for? All the cocks have been butchered. Tomorrow morning has been cancelled.
SHALL I
AS IS THE CUSTOM STICK A PIECE OF IRON INTO
THE NEAREST FLESH OR THE SECOND BEST
TO LATCH UNTO IT SINCE THE WORLD IS SPINNING
LORD BREAK MY NECK WHILE I'M FALLING FROM AN
ALEHOUSE BENCH

Enters Horatio. Confidant of my thoughts so full of blood since the morning is curtained by the empty sky. YOU'LL BE TOO LATE MY FRIEND FOR YOUR PAY-CHECK/NO PART FOR YOU IN THIS MY TRAGEDY. Horatio, do you know me? Are you my friend, Horatio? If you know me how can you be my friend? Do you want to play Polonius who wants to sleep with his daughter, the delightful Ophelia, here she enters right on cue, look how she shakes her ass, a tragic character. HoratioPolonius. I knew you're an actor. I am too, I'm playing Hamlet. Denmark is a prison, a wall is growing between the two of us. Look what's growing from that wall. Exit Polonius. My mother the bride. Her breasts a rosebed, her womb the snakepit. Have you forgotten your lines, Mama. I'll prompt you. WASH THE MURDER OFF YOUR FACE MY PRINCE/AND OFFER THE NEW DEN-MARK YOUR GLAD EYE. I'll change you back into a virgin mother, so your king will have a bloodwedding. A MOTHER'S WOMB IS NOT A ONE-WAY STREET. Now, I tie your hands on your back with your bridal veil since I'm sick of your embrace. Now, I tear the wedding dress. Now, I smear the shreds of the wedding dress with the dust my father turned into, and with the soiled shreds your face your belly your breasts. Now, I take you, my mother, in his, my father's invisible tracks. I stifle your scream with my lips. Do you recognize the fruit of your womb? Now go to your wedding, whore, in the broad Danish sunlight which shines on the living and the dead. I want to cram the corpse down the latrine so the palace will choke in royal shit. Then let me eat your heart, Ophelia, which weeps my tears.

2

THE EUROPE OF WOMEN

Enormous room. * *Ophelia. Her heart is a clock.*

OPHELIA (CHORUS/HAMLET):

I am Ophelia. The one the river didn't keep. The woman dangling from the rope. The woman with her arteries cut open. The woman with the overdose. SNOW ON HER LIPS. The woman with her head in the gas stove. Yesterday I stopped killing myself. I'm alone with my breasts my thighs my womb. I smash the tools of my captivity, the chair the table the bed. I destroy the battlefield that was my home. I fling open the doors so the wind gets in and the scream of the world. I smash the window. With my bleeding hands I tear the photos of the men I loved and who used me on the bed on the table on the chair on the ground. I set fire to my prison. I throw my clothes into the fire. I wrench the clock that was my heart out of my breast. I walk into the street clothed in my blood.

3

SCHERZO

The university of the dead. Whispering and muttering. From their gravestones (lecterns), the dead philosophers throw their books at Hamlet. Gallery (ballet) of the dead women. The woman dangling from the rope. The woman with her arteries cut open, etc. . . . Hamlet views them with the attitude of a visitor in a museum (theatre). The dead women tear his clothes off his body. Out of an up-ended coffin, labeled HAMLET 1, step Claudius and Ophelia, the latter dressed and made up like a whore. Striptease by Ophelia.

OPHELIA: Do you want to eat my heart, Hamlet? *Laughs.*

HAMLET: *Face in his hands.* I want to be a woman.
Hamlet dresses in Ophelia's clothes, Ophelia puts the make-up of a whore on his face, Claudius—now Hamlet's father—laughs without uttering a sound, Ophelia blows Hamlet a kiss and steps with Claudius/HamletFather back into the coffin. Hamlet poses as a whore. An angel, his face at the back of his head: Horatio. He dances with Hamlet.

VOICE(S): *From the coffin.* What thou killed thou shalt love.
The dance grows faster and wilder. Laughter from the coffin. On a swing, the madonna with breast cancer. Horatio opens an umbrella, embraces Hamlet. They freeze under the umbrella, embracing. The breast cancer radiates like a sun.

4

PEST IN BUDA / BATTLE FOR GREENLAND

Space 2, as destroyed by Ophelia. An empty armor, an ax stuck in the helmet.
HAMLET:
The stove is smoking in quarrelsome October
A BAD COLD HE HAD OF IT JUST THE WORST TIME*
JUST THE WORST TIME OF THE YEAR FOR A REVOLUTION*
Cement in bloom walks through the slums
Doctor Zhivago weeps
For his wolves
SOMETIMES IN WINTER THEY CAME INTO THE VILLAGE
AND TORE APART A PEASANT
He takes off make-up and costume.

THE ACTOR PLAYING HAMLET:

I'm not Hamlet. I don't take part any more. My words have nothing to tell me anymore. My thoughts suck the blood out of the images. My drama doesn't happen anymore. Behind me the set is put up. By people who aren't interested in my drama, for people to whom it means nothing. I'm not interested in it anymore either. I won't play along anymore. *Unnoticed by the actor playing Hamlet, stagehands place a refrigerator and three TV-sets on the stage. Humming of the refrigerator. Three TV-channels without sound.* The set is a monument. It presents a man who made history, enlarged a hundred times. The petrification of a hope. His name is interchangeable, the hope has not been fulfilled. The monument is toppled into the dust, razed by those who succeeded him in power three years after the state funeral of the hated and most honored leader. The stone is inhabited. In the spacy nostrils and auditory canals, in the creases of skin and uniform of the demolished monument, the poorer inhabitants of the capital are dwelling. After an appropriate period, the uprising follows the toppling of the monument. My drama, if it still would happen, would happen in the time of the uprising. The uprising starts with a stroll. Against the traffic rules, during the working hours. The street belongs to the pedestrians. Here and there, a car is turned over. Nightmare of a knife thrower: Slowly driving down a one-way street towards an irrevocable parking space surrounded by armed pedestrians. Policemen, if in the way, are swept to the curb. When the procession approaches the government district it is stopped by a police line. People form groups, speakers arise from them. On the balcony of a government building, a man in badly fitting mufti appears and begins to speak too. When the first stone hits him, he retreats behind the double doors of bullet-proof glass. The call for more freedom turns into the cry for the overthrow of the government. People begin to disarm the policemen, to storm two, three buildings, a prison a police precinct an office of the secret police, they string up a dozen henchmen of the rulers by their heels, the government brings in troops, tanks. My place, if my drama would still happen, would be on both sides of the front, between the frontlines, over and above them. I stand in the stench of the crowd and hurl stones at policemen soldiers tanks bullet-proof glass. I look through the double doors of bullet-proof glass at the crowd pressing forward and smell the sweat of my fear. Choking with nausea, I shake my fist at myself who stands behind the bullet-proof glass. Shaking with fear and contempt, I see myself in the crowd pressing forward, foaming at the mouth, shaking my fist at myself. I string up my uniformed flesh by my own heels. I am the soldier in the gun turret, my head is empty under the helmet, the stifled scream under the tracks. I am the typewriter. I tie the noose when the ringleaders are strung up, I pull the stool from under their feet, I break my own neck. I am my own prisoner. I feed my own data into the computers. My parts are the spittle and the spittoon the knife and the wound the fang and the throat the neck and the rope. I am the data bank. Bleeding in the crowd. Breathing again behind the double doors. Oozing wordslime in my soundproof blurb over and above the battle. My drama didn't happen. The script has been lost. The actors put their faces on the rack in the dressing room. In his box, the prompter is rotting. The stuffed corpses in the house don't stir a hand. I go home and kill the time, at one/with my undivided self.

Television The daily nausea Nausea

Of prefabricated babble Of decreed cheerfulness
How do you spell GEMÜTLICHKEIT
Give us this day our daily murder
Since thine is nothingness Nausea
Of the lies which are believed
By the liars and nobody else
Nausea
Of the lies which are believed Nausea
Of the mugs of the manipulators marked
By their struggle for positions votes bank accounts
Nausea A chariot armed with scythes sparkling with punchlines
I walk through streets stores Faces
Scarred by the consumers battle Poverty
Without dignity Poverty without the dignity
Of the knife the knuckleduster the clenched fist
The humiliated bodies of women
Hope of generations
Stifled in blood cowardice stupidity
Laughter from dead bellies
Hail Coca Cola
A kingdom
For a murderer
I WAS MACBETH
THE KING HAD OFFERED HIS THIRD MISTRESS TO ME
I KNEW EVERY MOLE ON HER HIPS
RASKOLNIKOV CLOSE TO THE
HEART UNDER THE ONLY COAT THE AX FOR THE
ONLY
SKULL OF THE PAWNBROKER
In the solitude of airports
I breathe again I am
A privileged person My nausea
Is a privilege
Protected by torture
Barbed wire Prisons
Photograph of the author.
I don't want to eat drink breathe love a woman a man a child an animal anymore.
I don't want to die anymore. I don't want to kill anymore.
Tearing of the author's photograph.
I force open my sealed flesh. I want to dwell in my veins, in the marrow of my bones, in the maze of my skull. I retreat into my entrails. I take my seat in my shit, in my blood. Somewhere bodies are torn apart so I can dwell in my shit. Somewhere bodies are opened so I can be alone with my blood. My thoughts are lesions in my brain. My brain is a scar. I want to be a machine. Arms for grabbing Legs to walk on, no pain no thoughts.

TV screens go black. Blood oozes from the refrigerator. Three naked women:

Marx, Lenin, Mao. They speak simultaneously, each one in his own language, the text:

THE MAIN POINT IS TO OVERTHROW ALL EXISTING CONDITIONS . . .*

The Actor of Hamlet puts on make-up and costume.

HAMLET THE DANE PRINCE AND MAGGOT'S FODDER
STUMBLING FROM HOLE TO HOLE TOWARDS THE FINAL
HOLE LISTLESS IN HIS BACK THE GHOST THAT ONCE
MADE HIM GREEN LIKE OPHELIA'S FLESH IN CHILDBED
AND SHORTLY ERE THE THIRD COCK'S CROW A CLOWN
WILL TEAR THE FOOL'S CAP OFF THE PHILOSOPHER
A BLOATED BLOODHOUND'LL CRAWL INTO THE ARMOR

He steps into the armor, splits with the ax the heads of Marx, Lenin, Mao. Snow. Ice Age.

5

FIERCELY ENDURING
MILLENIUMS
IN THE FEARFUL ARMOR
The deep sea. Ophelia in a wheelchair. Fish, debris, dead bodies and limbs drift by.
OPHELIA:
While two men in white smocks wrap gauze around her and the wheelchair, from bottom to top.
This is Electra speaking. In the heart of darkness. Under the sun of torture. To the capitals of the world. In the name of the victims. I eject all the sperm I have received. I turn the milk of my breasts into lethal poison. I take back the world I gave birth to. I choke between my thighs the world I gave birth to. I bury it in my womb. Down with the happiness of submission. Long live hate and contempt, rebellion and death. When she walks through your bedrooms carrying butcher knives you'll know the truth.
The men exit. Ophelia remains on stage, motionless in her white wrappings.

END

---

* English-language productions could use the entire quote from Karl Marx: Introduction to *Critique of Hegel's Philosophy of Law.*

Gundling's Life Frederick of Prussia Lessing's Sleep Dream Scream

A Horror Story

GUNDLING'S LIFE FREDERICK OF PRUSSIA LESSING'S SLEEP
DREAM SCREAM (*Leben Gundling's Friedrich von Preussen Lessings Schlaf
Traum Schrei*) was written in 1976 and first published in *Spektakulum 26*,
Suhrkamp Verlag, Frankfurt/Main 1977. The first production was staged by Horst
Laube at the Schauspielhaus, Frankfurt/Main, on January 26, 1979.

The way the play is constructed from splinters of numerous historical and
literary events, and its treatment of Prussian history as a continuing tradition of
political and spiritual repression assumes a reader and/or an audience thoroughly
familiar with Prusso-German history and culture from the early eighteenth century
to the present. However, even when read without such knowledge the text amounts
to a compelling indictment of the intellectual's misery in German history. The intellectuals of the play are not only the "professionals," like Gundling, Lessing,
Kleist, Schiller, etc. but Frederick the Second as well.

An interesting section is the American dream scene: Lessing and his "creatures"
Nathan and Emilia Galotti, the protagonists in two of his most famous plays, encounter the last American president who is a faceless robot, before they're all
destroyed by the "white light" of what seems to be a nuclear explosion. The text
contains allusions to the American Indian movement and other aspects of contemporary American society. The scene is followed by the ultimate emasculation of the
intellectual: Lessing's petrifaction as a classic.

A footnote: Lessing, like Müller, was born in Saxony, in January 1729, two hundred years before Müller, who was 47 years old when he wrote LESSING'S
SLEEP DREAM SCREAM, as the Lessing in the text.

C.W.

GUNDLING'S LIFE

Garden in Potsdam. A dining table. Frederick William with the boy Frederick in Lieutenant's uniform, Officers, Gundling. Beer and tobacco. A moon.

GUNDLING . . . and the wisdom of Your Majesty's decree about the suppression of foreign newspapers within Your Majesty's territory is evident from the mere fact that the universe as created by a God can *a priori* have only one center which is situated in Prussia, as it were with Your permission, beneath the Royal behind of His Most Gracious Majesty by Divine Grace Frederick William. *Frederick William farts. Frederick demonstratively holds his nose.* Thus God has created the universe. Which firstly is gaseous . . .

FREDERICK It still stinks.

FREDERICK WILLIAM How dare he, lout. I shall teach him manners, the French frog. To turn up his nose at his father's farts! Has he no family considerations. He is not in Versailles where everything is higgedly-piggedly. Did I turn up my nose when he was laying in his shit? A Prussian honors his family, come rain or shine. Sit straight, I say. And hands on the table. Is he playing at trousers again. The hands of the soldier are placed at the seam of the trouser leg, at dinner, on the tabletop. *Frederick crosses his arms in front.* Is he hiding his flute, scoundrel. *Snatches the flute from Frederick's tunic and breaks it across his knee.* He shall get the position, Gundling, 200 Thalers a year. He is a patriot. Will he pay his dues? I must feed a people, I have to be stingy. And cut 200 Thalers out of my own flesh for him because I love the sciences. *Gundling puts money on the table. Servants bring beer.* To the new president of the Royal Academy, Jacob Paul Baron Von Gundling. *Frederick William, Officers, Gundling drink.*

OFFICER 1 Has he only one title, Gundling?

GUNDLING *puts money on the table.* I wish I had none.

Beer. Officers drink.

OFFICER 2 That was the Counsellor of Appeals. What about the Master of Ceremonies?

OFFICER 3 And the Supreme Court Judge.

OFFICER 4 And the Privy Councillor.

Frederick William laughs. Gundling empties his pockets onto the table, etc.

OFFICER 1 Gundling, who made his horns sprout?

OFFICER 2 Did his spouse read him the riot act since he was drunk again?

GUNDLING The fate of the philosophers, gentlemen. I merely remind you of Socrates, the father of philosophy.

OFFICER 1 So it was his father who made his horns sprout.

Frederick William holds Frederick's ears shut.

OFFICER 2 Better the father does it to the son than the son to the father.

Officers laugh.

OFFICER 3 He who doesn't honor the father doesn't deserve the mother.

Officers laugh.

OFFICER 4 Gundling, we have a present for him. Is he a man?

GUNDLING *gets up, unsteady, reaches for his fly.* I can prove it.

Frederick William covers Frederick's eyes.

OFFICER 1 Here comes his proof.

Enter a bear. His paws are clipped, his teeth extracted. Gundling runs once around the table, pursued by the bear. The officers stop Gundling with their swords. The bear embraces Gundling.

OFFICER 2 The bride is aflame.

OFFICER 3 A skin like cream and roses.

OFFICER 4 Does he relish the embrace?

FREDERICK *hopefully.* Will he tear him apart, Papa?

FREDERICK WILLIAM *laughs*. He should take it as a lesson in what to make of philosophers. And in the art of government which he must learn when I go home to my maker, as the court preacher calls it, or into my nothingness. Clip the paws of the people, those animals, and pull their teeth. Ridicule the intellectuals so the rabble won't get ideas. He should take note of it, the bookworm, with his powder puff- and tragedy-nonsense. I want him to grow up a man. Is he biting his nails again? I'll show him.

Gundling falls flat on his back from the bear's embrace. Bear takes a bow, servants lead him away by his chain.

GUNDLING *on his back*. I wish I could lay on the dungheap behind my father's barn. *Officers laugh*. In England, I used to debate with Archbishops in Latin. England. O WHAT A NOBLE MIND IS HERE O'ERTHROWN.* *Officers laugh*. Observe, my learned students, the majesty of the firmament. And let this give you comfort: it too will pass away. Man is an accident, a malignant growth. And what we call life, Your Majesties, is something like the measles, the teething troubles of the universe whose true nature is death, nothingness, the void. Onward, Prussia!

FREDERICK WILLIAM *sternly*. Gundling, is he having ideas again.

OFFICER 1 It's delirium.

OFFICER 2 I'll pour him another one.

OFFICER 3 A waste of beer.—Here comes the fire brigade.

Officers piss on Gundling.

OFFICER 4 Nectar and ambrosia. The Lord gives it to His flock in their slumber.

FREDERICK WILLIAM *to Frederick*. Didn't you grow one, Prince?

FREDERICK I can't, Papa.

FREDERICK WILLIAM Ha. A Prussian officer and he can't piss, when his King gives the order. Is he a man? Demote the rascal! And unbutton his fly.

Officers rip the epaulettes off Frederick's tunic. Frederick cries.

OFFICERS Haha. He is pissing through his eyes.

---

*English in the original.

PRUSSIAN GAMES

1

Frederick, his sister Wilhelmina, Lieutenant Katte are playing blind man's buff. While Katte gropes about blindfolded, Frederick and Wilhelmina exchange their clothes. Frederick and Wilhelmina try to push each other aside as Katte approaches one of them. Sometimes, their touching turns into fondling, their pushing into an embrace. Katte comes upon Frederick, he holds him, feels his (Wilhelmina's) clothes, the wig, forehead eyes mouth.

KATTE *uncertain.* Wilhelmina.

Frederick stands stock still, only his hands twitch. As he reaches for Katte, Wilhelmina calls.

WILHELMINA Wrong wrong wrong. I am here.

Runs up to Katte from behind, leaning heavily against him she takes the blindfold off his eyes.

FREDERICK *ignoring Wilhelmina, offended, says to Katte* Let's play tragedy. I shall be Phedre. *Wilhelmina, feeling offended in her turn, withdraws into a corner from where she will step forward now and then to slap the hands of Frederick or Katte, whenever one tries to touch the other.*
Yes, Prince, I pine, I burn for Theseus.
. . .
With you I was saved and lost as well.

KATTE What do I hear, ye Gods! . . .
. . .
FREDERICK Give me your sword if you refuse the arm.
        Give.*

Frederick points Katte's sword at his own breast. Wilhelmina steps from her corner, wearing a crude mask of Frederick William, and in the gait and carriage of her Royal father she thrashes Frederick and Katte with a cane. Frederick and Katte tie her to a chair with shreds from her (Frederick's) clothes. Frederick points Katte's sword between her exposed breasts.

Die, mon cher Papa!
Laughter of Frederick and Katte.

2

Frederick, blindfolded, is led in by Soldiers; from the other side Lieutenant Katte, his eyes uncovered, yet he is in chains. Behind Frederick the firing squad for Katte

---

*Quotation from Racine's *Phedre*, Act II,5.

takes its position. Between Frederick and Katte, the King (Frederick William) takes his seat on a chair which two lackeys carry in after him.

FREDERICK WILLIAM Make your peace with your father in heaven, you dog. I'll help him up to the place, his Commander-in-Chief and Royal father, who has been punished by the Lord with him.

FREDERICK *trembling, softly.* Dog of a father.

FREDERICK WILLIAM Bitching again. I shall teach him to fuck assholes and to prattle in French. Stand straight. I want to make a man of him and a King. Even if I have to break every bone in his body to do it.

KATTE My Prince.

FREDERICK I see you.

At a signal from Frederick William, soldiers take Frederick's blindfold off. At the same time, Katte is blindfolded.

KATTE I am dying for the most noble of Princes.

FREDERICK *covers his eyes with his hands.* I cannot see you.

FREDERICK WILLIAM Show him the merry making.

SOLDIERS I am Santa Claus. *They pull Frederick's hands from his eyes, force his eyes open.*
Execution of Katte.
FREDERICK WILLIAM *gets up.* That was Katte.

FREDERICK Sire, that was I.

3

PROJECTION (Speaker)
  BUT THERE IS NOTHING WORSE THAN MAN; BE CONVINCED OF
  THIS MY DEAR (Frederick II)

FREDERICK *thrashes fleeing soldiers back into battle.* Dogs. Do you want to live forever.

SOLDIERS Our Fritz. Vivat Fridericus Rex Hurrah.
Soldiers die.
FREDERICK I wish I were my father.—Red snow. *Frederick throws up.* Read to me, Catt. *Catt opens a folding chair, Frederick sits down. His back to the battle, he faces the audience.*

CATT Plutarch?

FREDERICK Racine.
While the battle continues, Catt reads from Racine's Brittanicus, *IV.*

OH HOW GOOD THAT NO ONE KNOWS
RUMPELSTILTSKIN IS MY NAME
or
THE SCHOOL OF THE NATION
A patriotic puppet play

A wall of fire, in front a snowstorm. Through the snow, soldiers (puppets) in German Wehrmacht uniforms are goose-stepping into the fire. Downstage right at the footlights, a blackboard on which Frederick II is writing grades for the soldiers who hobble crawl or are carried back from the battle: F (Fail) for those who have no wounds or only light ones, better grades (C,B) for every serious wound or loss of limbs, A (Outstanding) for the dead.

FREDERICK On meadows all green
           Flowers in bloom
           Yellow for pigs
           Blue for the kids
           Red for my love
           White for the dead.

On the other side of the stage, larger-than-life figures of John Bull and Marianne divide the world by throwing knives at a globe, knives they are pulling from corpses of dead Indians and Negroes. After each hit, the winner cuts a slice off and ingests it. Having eaten their fill, they rub their (sometimes each other's) bellies, and burping and farting they watch little Frederick who is playing at war with his soldier-dolls. As the snowstorm grows worse and the fire is extinguished, the scene freezes. The stage is changed to a ghost-ship, dead sailors are nailing the captain to the main mast. The film runs in reverse, forward again, in reverse again. And so forth, through the centuries. Music: Handel's "THE MUSICAL SACRIFICE."

KING OF HEARTS   BLACK WIDOW

Projection Leda with the swan (Rubens). Frederick pulls from a cabinet a Prussian doll with the mask of Frederick William, he rocks caresses kisses it in front of a mirror.

FREDERICK My people.
Slaps the face of the doll, throws it on the floor, dances on top of it.
Bastard.
Throws the doll back into the cabinet, sits on a chair, pokes his nose. A stocky Lady from Saxony in black veils rushes in. Frederick takes the finger out of his nose and hides his hand behind the chair.

SAXON LADY I am the widow.

FREDERICK *jumps up.*
> What kind of a widow.

SAXON LADY *crowding him.*
Or the most happy of all females if
Your Majesty wills it.

FREDERICK *flees.*
Majesty won't.

SAXON LADY *pursues him across the room.*
Namely my husband, father of my children
Eight altogether, is that officer
Of the Saxonian army who while pris'ner
Of war accepted a Prussian commission
A Prussian now and of late a deserter
Out of pure love, since home to Saxony
His full and noble heart was drawing him
—*Hand on her heart*—
To shoot him was Your Majesty's decree
Early today according to the rules of war
The same man's widow I, if not Your Grace
Will show him mercy which I'm begging for
Here on my knees, or wife again, if you.
Throwing herself on her knees, she grabs for Frederick's legs.

FREDERICK *escapes.*
You are the widow, His Majesty won't.

SAXON LADY Aah.
*Faints. Frederick circles in wide curves around the unconscious woman. The Saxon
Lady comes to, throws her arms up.*
> Mercy!

FREDERICK *withdraws to a safe distance.*
> The heavens are empty, Madame!
The Saxon Lady gets up, reaches out for him.
And I, I am the king.

SAXON LADY   Have you a heart?

FREDERICK *statesman like.*
Not for myself.
Walking up and down the room.
> Your husband, for example,
A man of honor, of Saxony his honor.
So, what is Prussia's honor to him which I,

The King of Prussia, am the guardian of.
And should my heart break of it. An open wound,
Madame, that's what a king's heart is.

SAXON LADY *weeps.*
                    Your Majesty.

FREDERICK *sings.*
Oh, Madame, if you only knew, oh, of my
Lonesome nights.

SAXON LADY *steps towards him, opening her arms wide.*
                    And mine, Your Majesty.

FREDERICK *steps back, draws his sword.*
Ah, how this breast is longing for this comfort!—
You crowned heads! You, Europe in decay!
You'll all see this example, how a king dies!
Tries to point the sword at his breast, his arms are too short, the sword is too long,
he hits his crotch.

SAXON LADY *takes the sword.*
No, Majesty, you're not allowed. My husband

FREDERICK If I'd be allowed. She's right: I am not.
Of all the Prussians I'd be most happy
If someone else would be the King of Prussia.
How envious am I of my victim's death
They are allowed to die, but I must kill.

SAXON LADY I am disconsolate. Majesty. My husband

FREDERICK If I could take his place.

SAXON LADY *closes her eyes.*
                    Oh Majesty.

FREDERICK An honorable man. He has one honor
Only, a Saxon honor, and what is that,
Honor of Saxony, to my good Prussians.
They screw their mothers up against the wall
For Prussia's honor, and won't bat an eyelash.
And what's an hon'rable deserter to me,
He's to my braves simply a Saxon blemish
Which ought to be wiped off for a clean Prussia.
Did ever you have the occasion, Madame,
You'll have it soon, to be the witness of

An execution. An ugly show to watch.
Saxon lady bawls, Frederick steps up to the mirror.
Oh, what a wondrous work of art is man.
Covers his eyes with his hands, peeps through the fingers, turns away from the mirror.
If nature wouldn't have created him
I
A short glance at the mirror.
 And what's he like with twenty bullets.
Better we drop this. Man has one mistake:
The world were Prussian if my Prussians didn't
Gobble and booze and whore and shit like swine
Better we drop this. God's a pig. If he
Exists. Do you believe, Madame?

SAXON LADY   I pray.

FREDERICK Better pray fast.
Looks out of the window/into the audience.
                    A picture of a man.
And it is here in front of this my window
That it's destroyed.
Takes the veil off the lady's face and covers his own face with it.
                    Was he good in bed,
Widow?
Saxon lady bawls. Frederick dances.
                    I am the widow-maker. Making
Women into widows, that's my trade
I empty all the beds and fill the graves.
Laughs, lets the veil drop.
Now you can play with your own body, widow.
Shudders.
Until a new belly will rub your belly.
Weeps.
That I must see it. Here. With these my eyes.
Grandly.
Am I allowed to close my eyes when my word
Becomes brute force? If I were blind. Ah
Picks up the veil and blindfolds himself with it.

SAXON LADY   Poor king.

FREDERICK Did you say mercy? Do you want the King
Never look into my eyes again
And into those of my dear Prussians who rush
To every death for me, run the gauntlet,
And so forth. Into the eyes of mothers

Who butcher all their sons for him, their King.
And into history's eye which won't ignore him
Not even for a single second. Can you
Want that?
Saxon lady vehemently shakes her head.
        And yet, what's Prussia, what's the King,
What's history, I'll throw it all away
If you say so.
Kneels on one knee.
        Madame, I'll offer you
My fame if you want it, for your small happiness.

SAXON LADY How could I, Majesty! Oh, my great King!
Lifts Frederick from the floor, takes off the blindfold, wipes his face dry with the veil, covers her own face again with the veil, places the chair at the window, facing the audience, sits down, takes Frederick on her lap, rocks him and sings.
HAPPY HE
WHO FORGETS
WHAT ANYHOW CANNOT BE CHANGED
Drums. Noise of the firing squad marching into position.

FREDERICK *jumps from the lady's lap.*
Madame, the time has come.
Looks out through the window/into the audience, covers his eyes with his hands.
        I cannot look.
If you'll permit.
He hides behind the Saxon lady, his head pops up to peek from behind. The Saxon lady folds back her veil, stares with eyes wide open through the window/into the audience. Volley. Frederick jumps on the woman's back simultaneously. Frederick on top of the woman.
        Did you see. It squirts.
Chokes her with the veil. The Saxon lady throws her arms up, topples over with chair and Frederick.
My Royal sympathy.

SAXON LADY   My children.

FREDERICK *with an eagle mask.*
My cannons need their fodder, breed it, mare.
Why else was your sex given you? To share.
Saxon Lady leaves quickly.

OH DEAR LORD MAKE ME WELL
SINCE I'M COMING STRAIGHT FROM HELL

Prussian insane asylum. War cripples are playing at war. Veterans are exercising

*the goose-step and run the gauntlet. A hunt for rats. A Man in a cage. A Child with
a bandage. A Woman in a stupor.*

WOMAN *sings.*
  Once there were three murderers
  Oh rose abloom
  Who claimed they were three counts of blood
  Mountain valley snow so cold
  Leaving your love hurts hundred-fold

  They come to Mrs. Publican's inn
  Oh rose abloom
  Can you put up three counts one night
  Mountain valley snow so cold
  Leaving your love hurts hundred-fold

  Oh yes and barn and stable are free
  Oh rose abloom
  Couldn't I put up three counts one night
  Mountain valley snow so cold
  Leaving your love hurts hundred-fold

  The first puts the horse into the stable
  Oh rose abloom
  The second deals out the oats for it
  Mountain valley snow so cold
  Leaving your love hurts hundred-fold

  The third jumped through the kitchen door
  Oh rose abloom
  And kissed the Publican's daughter there
  Mountain valley snow so cold
  Leaving your love hurts hundred-fold

  The first one said the girl is mine
  Oh rose abloom
  I've bought and brought her a bottle of wine
  Mountain valley snow so cold
  Leaving your love hurts hundred-fold

  The second said the girl is mine
  Oh rose abloom
  I've bought and brought her a ring so fine
  Mountain valley snow so cold
  Leaving your love hurts hundred-fold

The third one said we don't deserve the maid
Oh rose abloom
We have to kill her with our blade
Mountain valley snow so cold
Leaving your love hurts hundred-fold

They sat the girl on the table top
Oh rose abloom
Stabbed seventy times before they stopp'd
Mountain valley snow so cold
Leaving your love hurts hundred-fold

And where a drop of blood did spill
Oh rose abloom
An angel from heaven was sitting still
Mountain valley snow so cold
Leaving your love hurts hundred-fold*

Professor with students.

PROFESSOR A murderess. From adultery to marital murder—only one step. The husband was a Supreme Court justice. She owes her presence in our institution to the sad fact that the executioner was drunk. Our great King gave the potato to Prussia. And how does his brave landed gentry thank him for it.

STUDENT With potato schnapps. *Students laugh.*

PROFESSOR She was pardoned after the third try. You see the three scars on her neck. And so she is standing before us, an unfinished person. *The woman rips her clothes off her body. Attendants with strait-jacket. A struggle.* The strait-jacket. An instrument of dialectics, as my colleague of the Philosophical faculty would conclude. A school of freedom indeed. You need only look, to be understood as the inevitability of necessity. The more the patient struggles, the tighter he straps himself, he himself, mark my words, into his own destiny. Everyone is his own Prussian, to use a popular phrase. Here lies the educational value, the humanism so to speak, of the strait-jacket which could be just as easily called the freedom jacket. The philosopher would conclude that true freedom is based on catatonia as the most complete expression of the discipline which made Prussia great. The consequences are very attractive: the ideal state founded on the stupor of its populace, eternal peace on the universal stoppage of the bowels. The physician knows: States are based on the sweat of their peoples, the temple of reason on pillars of feces.

STUDENT To use a popular phrase. *Students laugh.*

---

*German folk song from the sixteenth century, maybe older.

PROFESSOR I have to insist on a more scientific attitude, gentlemen. See this boy, turned into an idiot through masturbation. The ruin of a blooming childhood. *Boy shows them his tongue.* And the triumph of science: the masturbation bandage I have invented. As you can see, a construction as simple as it is ingenious, which makes pliable even the most hardboiled little sinner if consistently applied. *Boy spits. Attendants gag him.* It can be adjusted according to size and if I may add a footnote, gentlemen, please permit this patriotic digression: I for my part don't believe it is an accident that this my modest invention is applied particularly in the enlightened Prussia of our virtuous King. A victory of reason over the raw instincts. Against which even the daily application of the cane couldn't prevail: As soon as he stopped feeling the cane on his back—even the best pedagogue's punishing hand will tire eventually; man, unfortunately, is not a machine—the impenitent didn't wait for his welts to heal but immediately went to repeat the shameful manipulation of the tool which our creator has reserved for procreation, in Christian wedlock, of course, that goes without saying. Even he is in God's image, He created him in His own likeness, to quote a certain theologian. *Students laugh.* I won't mention his name. *Students laugh.* Blasphemy. Imagine Our Lord masturbating, deus masturbator. *Students laugh.*

STUDENT Or a certain theologian.

PROFESSOR *laughs.* After four weeks with this bandage that works, so to speak, like an extended, and because mechanical, tireless arm of pedagogy, even the most wicked libertine will forget his sex. May I demonstrate. *Attendants take off the bandage. Boy, his face distorted with pain, rubs his numbed arms, rips off his muzzle, and reaches for his genitals. Students laugh. Furious.* An idiot.—Put him in fetters.—The bandage wasn't tight enough. Sheer negligence. *Boy is put in fetters, he bawls.*

STUDENT 1 I propose amputation, Professor, Sir.

STUDENT 2 Castration.

STUDENT 3 Twice done is better than one. *Students laugh.*

PROFESSOR A dashing proposal, dear colleague. But not being a veterinary surgeon, I'd rather rely on my more modest method. A good thing needs time, young friend. The surgeon's knife is the ultima ratio.—Present him again in three weeks.

MAN IN CAGE I have butchered my son, my Jesus. Hand me the rod. Hand me the rod.

PROFESSOR Give it to him. *It is done. Man in the cage flagellates himself.* He calls this doing penance for the creation of the universe. Zebahl, Zebaoth, also called the Bloody Baal by those pupils who were entrusted to his punishing hand. A well trained hand, as you see, Corporal during the Seven Years War, a teacher according to the book. Jesus was his darling, he got the nickname from his classmates because he never took part in their pranks. Probably because Zebahl, as the wagging tongues maintained, had some part in his extramarital production. *Students laugh.* An angel, in any case, with whom the teacher shared his bedroom. *Students laugh.* The rest is in the Bible. *Students laugh.* When Zebaoth once inflicted a terrible judgment upon his pupils, Jesus offered himself as the sacrificial lamb. He wanted to take the punishment upon himself, one for all, the lamb of God. His creator, moved to tears by such virtue, accepted. And not to fall short of his own creature in magnanimity and to double the pedagogic effect, he did more than was asked for by leaving it to the sinners themselves to make the punishment an example for all. They did it thoroughly: Lord Zebaoth has no son anymore, the village a new school master, the history of Medicine a high point: God as a patient.

ZEBAHL I am ashamed. I am ashamed. I am ashamed.

STUDENT 1 I hear you've created the universe, Mr. Zebahl.

ZEBAHL Yes, it is my fault. Everything is my fault. I am omnipotent.

STUDENT 2 *crosses his hands in front of his genitals.* And I am the Virgin Mary.

STUDENT 3 I am Jesus. *Moving his arms like wings.* This is the ascension.

STUDENT 4 *sticks out his belly.* I am the Pope of Rome.
All four kneel in front of the cage.
OUR FATHER WHO ART IN HEAVEN
Students laugh.

PROFESSOR An insane asylum. Quod erat demonstrandum. Let's go, gentlemen. *Professor and students exit.*

ZEBAHL *whispers.* Yes, I created the world. I am the fool, I am the criminal. I can gouge my eyes out and yet I see you. If I could only die. I have butchered my son. I, the dung of my creation vomit of my angels putrid cyst in my harmonies. I am the slaughterhouse. I am the earthquake. I am the animal. The war. I am the desert. *A scream. Black angels invade the house and, without a sound, attack the audience.*

ET IN ARCADIA EGO:* THE INSPECTION

Turnip field. A peasant family is crawling in the furrows. Close to the footlights a lectern is placed, close to the field a block of marble. A Boys Choir is taking its place, their mouths wide open to sing. A flock of painters is setting up easels.

---

*"I too was in Arcadia." (Horace)

Friedrich Schiller steps behind the lectern, the sculptor Schadow goes to the block of marble. Enter Frederick of Prussia with his crooked walking stick, officials and Voltaire. Officials place two folding chairs. Frederick and Voltaire take their seats. Schiller, interrupted by fits of coughing, recites "THE PROMENADE." The sculptor Schadow works away at the block of marble, once in a while taking measure of the peasant woman when she raises herself in the furrow to stretch her back. When she cannot stoop anymore because of her stiff back, the peasant helps her stoop down into the furrow with a blow of his fist. Frederick assumes a Royal stance. The painters paint. The Boys Choir sings NO BETTER COUNTRY IN OUR AGE / THAN THIS HERE OURS WIDE AND FAR.

Frederick rises, strides, points, always Royally, and maintains his poses for a considerable time for the painters, yet with visible effort because of his gout, occasionally repeating a pose, or improving it, he gets ready to speak, looks indignantly at Schiller who is still reciting "THE PROMENADE" at the footlights though the Boys Choir has already fallen silent. Officials empty a sack of turnips and pull it over Schiller's head. During the following, we hear in intervals his muffled coughing.

FREDERICK Yes indeed: no spectacle affords more pleasure to a King's eye than a flourishing province peopled by an industrious peasantry going peacefully about its work. Farm produce prospers and so do the arts . . . Oh the meager beauty of my Prussia! I am not using the possessive pronoun as such, my dear Voltaire, rather I am considering the oneness-unité-of state and people which Prussia is setting as an example for the world. I am the people, if you know what I mean. *Applause of the officials. Frederick, addressing the peasant through a megaphone.* The oranges have turned out well this year, haven't they.

PEASANT *stands at attention, his family joins him.* Ay, ay, Your Majesty, these are turnips.

FREDERICK Did he say turnips.

PEASANT CHILDREN *(6)*
ONE TWO THREE FOUR FIVE SIX
A PEASANT WOMAN COOKS TURNIPS

FREDERICK We shall see. Taste it. *Throws a turnip to the peasant. The peasant eats the turnip.* Do his oranges taste well, lout?

PEASANT *spits out teeth.* The oranges taste well, yes, Majesty.

Voltaire throws up at the footlights.

FREDERICK *to the peasant.* Very good.—A peasant dance for our guest from France. *He is handed a flute. The officials put rooster's heads (masks) on the peasant, his wife and their children. Frederick plays a rebellious peasant dance tune. Voltaire stops his ears. Peasant family dances in the furrows. Applause, even by Voltaire. The peasants return the rooster's heads to the officials. To Voltaire.* An art-loving people, my Prussians. *To the peasant.* Try bananas next year. *Frederick turns to leave. A painter shows him his canvas. After a glance at the canvas, Frederick points with his crooked stick at the statue which by now has become recognizable: a classical female nude.* Art is beauty. Ten strokes for the dauber. *An official hits the painter over the head with the canvas, his colleagues paint his face black. General exit.* ET IN ARCADIA EGO. *Points at the audience.* Look at the cattle, grazing peacefully. Prussia, a home for people and cattle. And you can say, you were there, my dear Voltaire.

VOLTAIRE *picks up a turnip.* A souvenir. A Prussian orange.

Everbody exits. Only Schiller and the peasants remain on stage. The peasant crows, topples the statue over, and, with his fists, beats his wife and children to make them work faster. Bereft of his lectern, the sack still over his head, Schiller stands couging at the footlights.

FREDERICK THE GREAT

Suite of rooms converging on a narrow door at Sanssouci. * *Downstage the State Council: Creatures and councillors with papers. Sound of the heartbeat and breathing of the dying King. Whispering choir of the State Council, increasing:* He's croaking He's croaking He's croaking. *Heartbeat and breathing stop. Silence. Wind blows the papers from the hands of the councillors propels them across the stage swirls them around it. State Council members chase after the papers. More papers are blown on stage, into the audience. Curtain with the black eagle.*

HEINRICH VON KLEIST PLAYS MICHAEL KOHLHASS

Despoiled shore (a lake near Strassburg). Kleist in uniform. A doll of Kleist. A doll of a woman. A doll of a horse. Executioner's block. Kleist touches face breast hands genitals of the Kleist doll. Caresses kisses embraces the woman's doll. Cuts off the head of the horse's doll with his sword. Rips the heart from the woman's doll and eats it. Rips the uniform off his body, wraps the head of the Kleist doll in the tunic, puts on the horse's head, hacks the Kleist doll to pieces with his sword; roses and bowels spill from it. Throws off the horse's head, puts on the wig (hair down to the heels) of the woman's doll, breaks his sword over his knee, approaches the executioner's block. Takes off the wig, spreads the woman's hair over the executioner's block, bites open his artery, sawdust trickles from his arm which he holds over the woman's hair resting on the executioner's block. A white cloth is thrown from the flies onto the scene, a red spot quickly spreads on it.

---

*Frederick's palace near Potsdam.

LESSING'S SLEEP DREAM SCREAM

1

PROJECTION (Speaker)
THROUGHOUT HIS LIFE LESSING ENJOYED AN EXTREMELY OBE-
DIENT SLEEP WHICH DESCENDED AS SOON AS HE DECIDED TO
CLOSE HIS EYES HE OFTEN ASSURED ME THAT HE NEVER HAD
DREAMED THIS BLESSING STAYED WITH HIM UP TO HIS END AND
EVEN SHORTLY BEFORE HE TOLD ME THAT HE LOOKED FOR-
WARD TO THE NIGHT EVEN WHEN HE HAD SLEPT ALL DAY
(Leisewitz)

Actor is made up—Lessing's features—and dressed in costume. Stagehands set up a long table and chairs.

ACTOR *reads.* My name is Gotthold Ephraim Lessing. I am 47 years of age. I have stuffed one/two dozen dolls with sawdust that was my blood, have dreamed a dream of theatre in Germany, and reflected in public about things which were of no interest to me. That is over now. Yesterday, I discovered a dead spot on my skin, a piece of desert: Dying begins. Or rather: is accelerating. By the way, I happen to agree with it. One life is enough. I have seen one new age arise after another, each one dripping blood excrement sweat from all its pores. History arrives at the win-ning post on a dead horse. I have seen the hell of women from below: The woman dangling from the rope The woman with her arteries cut open The woman with the overdose SNOW ON HER LIPS The woman with her head in the gas oven. For thirty years, I have tried to keep myself from the chasm with words, consumptive from the dust of the archives and from the ashes which drift from the pages of books, choked by my growing disgust with literature, burned by my ever more fer-vent desire for silence. In the babble of the academies I have envied the deaf mutes for their silence. And in the beds of the many women I didn't love I envied their soundless fornication. I am beginning to forget my text. I am a sieve. More and more words fall through. Soon I shall hear no other voice but my own which asks for forgotten words. *Friends enter, debate soundlessly, occupy the chairs.* These are my friends. *Friends bow.* I started to forget their names for quite some time now. *Friends pull stocking masks over their faces.* To forget is to be wise. The Gods forget faster than anyone. It is good to sleep. Death is a woman.

Actor freezes in Lessing mask, friends in poses of debating.

2

PROJECTION (Speaker)
FROM THE PRUSSIA OF THE SECOND FREDERICK GOLD OF THE
GOOSE-STEP SILVER OF RUNNING THE GAUNTLET LESSING COMES
TO AMERICA LAND OF THE POTATO THAT WILL MAKE PRUSSIA
GREAT IN AN AUTOMOBILE JUNKYARD IN MONTANA HE EN-
COUNTERS THE LAST PRESIDENT OF THE USA

Auto junkyard. Electric chair, in it a robot without a face. In between under the car wrecks classical stage characters and film stars in various poses of accidental death. Music. "WELCOME MY SON WELCOME TO MACHINE" (Pink Floyd's "WISH YOU WERE HERE"). Lessing with Nathan the Wise and Emilia Galotti, the names on their costumes.

EMILIA GALOTTI *recites.* Force! Force! Who cannot resist force? What is called force is nothing: Seduction is the true force! I have blood, father, blood as young and as warm as anyone's. My senses too are senses. I vouch for nothing. I am good for nothing . . . Give me, my father, give me this dagger . . .

NATHAN *recites the ending of the Ring parable at the same time:* Well then . . .

Police siren. Emilia and Nathan exchange their heads, undress embrace kill each other. White light. Death of the machine on the electric chair. Stage goes black.

VOICE (+ PROJECTION)
HOUR OF WHITE HEAT DEAD BUFFALOS FROM THE CANYONS SQUADS OF SHARKS TEETH OF BLACK LIGHT THE ALLIGATORS MY FRIENDS GRAMMAR OF EARTHQUAKES WEDDING OF FIRE AND WATER MEN OF A NEW FLESH LAUTREAMONTMALDOROR PRINCE OF ATLANTIS SON OF THE DEAD

3

PROJECTION
APOTHEOSIS SPARTACUS A FRAGMENT

On stage a pile of sand covering a torso. Stagehands costumed as members of the audience pour sand from buckets and sacks on the pile, while simultaneously waiters fill the stage with busts of poets and philosophers. Lessing burrows in the sand, digging up a hand, an arm. The waiters, in hard hats now, fit a Lessing bust on Lessing, which covers his head and shoulders. On his knees, Lessing makes futile efforts to free himself of the bust. We can hear his muffled scream from under the bronze bust. Applause by waiters, stagehands (audience).

END

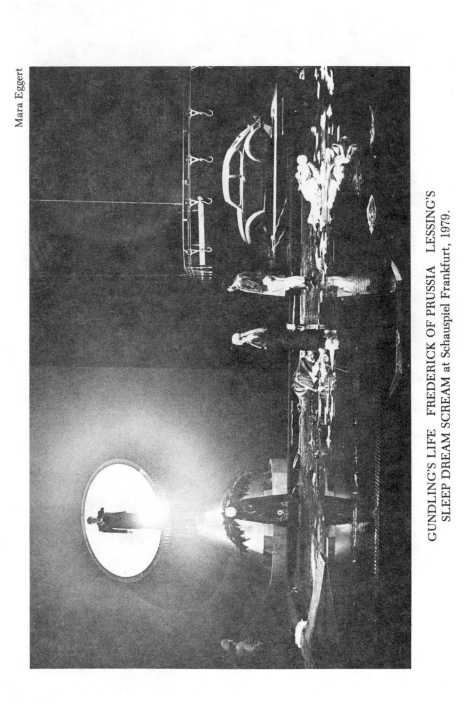

Mara Eggert

GUNDLING'S LIFE FREDERICK OF PRUSSIA LESSING'S
SLEEP DREAM SCREAM at Schauspiel Frankfurt, 1979.

Eva Kemlein

THE TASK, in the production directed by Heiner Müller and Ginka
Cholakova, at Volksbühne, East Berlin, 1980.

The Task

THE TASK (*Der Auftrag*) was written in 1979 and published in *Sinn und Form*, Nr. 6, Berlin 1979. The first production opened November 16, 1980, at the small 'Theatre im 3.Stock,' the studio space of the Volksbühne in Berlin, where an audience of forty could be seated. The production was directed by Heiner Müller in collaboration with his wife, Ginka Cholakova. In February 1982 Müller staged the text a second time, in a lavishly designed production for the Bochum Theatre in West Germany.

"The play uses themes from the story 'The Light on the Gallows' by Anna Seghers," Müller wrote in an author's note. This story obviously had already impressed Müller twenty years earlier. In 1958 he wrote the poem:

THEME OF A. S.

Debuisson in Jamaica
Between black breasts
In Paris Robespierre
His jaw broken.
Or Jeanne d'Arc when the angel failed to appear
The angels always fail to appear in the end
MOUNTAIN OF FLESH DANTON CAN'T GIVE
MEAT TO THE STREET
LOOK LOOK AT THE FLESH IN THE
STREET
THE HUNT FOR RED DEER IN THE YELLOW
SHOES.
Christ. The Devil showed him the kingdoms of the world
THROW OFF YOUR CROSS AND ALL WILL BE THINE.
In the time of treason
The landscapes are beautiful.

The poem expresses some of the ideas the play elaborated, and some of the poem's images appear in the text. (The line: "The hunt for red deer in the yellow shoes" refers to the Hungarian revolution of 1956 when members of the Secret Police were recognized by their yellow shoes, imported from the West, and recently issued to the force; many of those caught were strung up in the streets.)

Asked about the play's collage-like structure, Muller explained in a radio interview for Deutschlandfunk: "It results from my relation to the material—to each material. That's what determines the form or dramaturgy of my plays. This case might be special, i.e., the deviation from some dramaturgical norm is especially extreme since so many historical periods are mixed." The play's subtitle is "Memory of a Revolution," Müller explains: "The French Revolution . . . didn't interest me as much as a historical event, however it did as 'theatre,' as a revolutionary model that had an especially large arsenal of theatrical forms, among other reasons there was the relatively wide discrepancy between the intentions of the protagonists and the real mechanism, the real objectives . . . It is, of course, the only model for revolutions in Europe, or the—now as ever—classic model from which we can 'read' fairly accurately the progression and the wrong moves of other, subsequent revolutions. [The piece] is a mix of many things . . . biographical events are involved, a trip to Mexico among others that was very important for me in connection with the play."

The long segment in which the small-time official riding in an elevator misses his appointment with the boss, "Number One," the most Kafkaesque text ever published by Müller, is, according to the author, based on the "protocol of a dream." "It changed, of course, in the process of writing it down, something I can hardly control. At bottom, there is only one principle for me while I'm writing . . . When I start writing I know for sure that I'm going to finish it, provided I don't die before. And everything that comes to my mind while I'm writing is important and will be used some time at some place."

The term "Number One" in the elevator story reminds the reader of Arthur Koestler's novel *Darkness at Noon* where the term appears in connection with Stalin's person. Müller denies that he was aware of this when he wrote the text and feels a "Number One" is to be found in any social system: "Here [in the West] the power structures are at least as distinct, only maybe somewhat more subtle and complex, consequently more stable, whereas [in the East] they are more public."

Müller refuses to pass judgment on the decisions of the three revolutionary emissaries: "Fundamental positions are driven to certain conclusions; it isn't my job to decide in favor of one of them, neither in the text nor on the stage. That is the spectator's problem . . . which positions they'll accept as their own; or they can even reject all of them. The main point . . . is the difference between historical positions and standards. For Debuisson, the leader of the group, who has at least an upper-class background, this task isn't as existential as for the black man who doesn't have any other possibility at all, who doesn't have the option of treason."

C.W.

Galloudec to Antoine. I am writing this letter on my deathbed. I am writing in my own name and in the name of Citizen Sasportas who has been hanged at Port Royal. I am herewith informing you that we have to give back the task with which the Assembly asked your person to entrust us since we were unable to fulfill it. Maybe others will do better. You won't hear from Debuisson anymore, he is fine. It seems that traitors have a good time when the people walk in blood. That is the way the world is designed and it is not good. Excuse my handwriting, they have amputated one of my legs and I am writing in fever. I hope this letter will find you in good health, and I remain with Republican greetings.

Sailor. Antoine. Woman.

SAILOR Are you the Citizen Antoine. Then here is a letter for you. From someone called Galloudec. It isn't my fault if the letter is old, and maybe the matter is already settled. The Spanish detained us in Cuba, then the English in Trinidad, until your Consul Bonaparte made peace with England. Then they robbed me in London on the street because I was drunk, but they didn't find the letter. As for this Galloudec: he won't get any older. He croaked in a hospital in Cuba, half prison and half hospital. He was lying there with gangrene, I with fever. TAKE THE LETTER IT'S GOT TO ARRIVE AND IF IT'S THE LAST THING YOU DO YOU GOT TO DO THIS FOR ME was the last thing he said to me. And the address of an office and your name, if you are this Antoine. But there isn't an office anymore and of you, Antoine—if that is your name—nobody knows anything at the place where the office was. One guy who lives in a basement behind the scaffolding directed me to a school where an Antoine supposedly worked as a teacher. But there too they never heard of the man. Then a cleaning woman told me your nephew saw you here. He is a carter. And he described you to me, if you are the man.

ANTOINE I don't know any Galloudec.

SAILOR I don't know what in the letter was so important to him. Something about some task. Which he has to give back so that others can continue his work. Whatever work that was. In the end he didn't talk of anything else. Except when he howled and that was the pain. It came in waves. And it took long enough—until he was through with dying. The doctor said his heart was too strong, he ought to have been dead ten times over. Sometimes a man can endure too little, sometimes too much. Life is a rotten business. The other one he is writing about in his letter, a negro, had a speedier death. He read the letter to me, Galloudec, so that I know it by heart in case it got lost. And if you still don't know him, I'll tell you what they did to him and how he died. You weren't there. First, they cut off one of his legs up to the knee, then the rest of it. It was the left one. Then . . .

ANTOINE I don't know of any task. I don't assign tasks, I don't have the power. I earn my money with private lessons. It's little. And butcheries I have seen enough. I know the human anatomy inside out. Galloudec.

Woman with wine bread cheese.

WOMAN You have company. I've sold a medal. The one for the Vendée where you slaughtered the peasants for the Republic.

ANTOINE Yes.

SAILOR As far as I can see you still have everything. Unlike this Galloudec whom you don't know and who is dead as a stone. The other man's name was Sasportas. They have hanged him at Port Royal, if you want to know, because of the task you don't know anything of. In Jamaica. The gallows stand on a cliff. When they're dead they're cut down to drop into the sea below. The sharks take care of the rest. Thanks for the wine.

ANTOINE Sasportas. I am the Antoine you've been looking for. I've got to be careful. France isn't a Republic anymore, our Consul has become Emperor and is conquering Russia. It is easier to talk about a revolution lost when you've got a full mouth. Blood turned into the tin for medals. The peasants didn't know any better either, did they. And maybe they were right, weren't they. Commerce is thriving. We now feed the people in Haiti their own soil. That was 'the Negro Republic for you. Liberty leads the people to the barricades, and when the dead awaken she is in a uniform. Now I'll tell you a secret: she too is only a whore. And I am already able to laugh about it. Hahaha. But in here something is empty that was alive. I was there when the people stormed the Bastille. I was there when the head of the last of the Bourbons dropped into the basket. We have reaped the heads of the aristocrats. We have reaped the heads of the traitors.

WOMAN Nice harvest that. Are you drunk again, Antoine.

ANTOINE She doesn't like me to talk about my great time. The Gironde trembled before me. Look at her, my France. Her breasts dried up. Between her thighs the desert. A dead vessel in the surf of the new century. See how she gulps it down. France needs a bloodbath, and the day shall come.

Antoine pours red wine over his head.

SAILOR I don't understand anything of that. I'm a sailor, I don't believe in politics. The world is different wherever you go. Here is the letter.

Leaves.

ANTOINE *shouts.* Be careful, sailor, when you leave my house. The police of our minister Fouché won't ask you if you believe in politics.—Galloudec. Sasportas. Where is your leg, Galloudec. Why is your tongue dangling from your mouth, Sasportas. What do you want of me. Am I responsible for your stump. And for your rope. Shall I cut off one of my legs. Do you want me to hang myself next to you. Ask your Emperor, Galloudec, for your leg. Show your tongue to your Emperor, Sasportas. He is victorious in Russia, I can show you the way. What do you want of me. Go. Go away. Get lost. You tell them, woman. Tell them they should go away, I don't want to see them anymore. Are you still here. Your letter has arrived, Galloudec. This is it. Anyway, it's all over for you. LONG LIVE THE REPUBLIC. *Laughs.* You think I am fine, don't you. Are you hungry. There. *Throws food on the dead.*

WOMAN Come to bed, Antoine.

ANTOINE   NOW THE ASCENSION FOR A LITTLE CASH
            IN THE CHEST'S GRATING AS LONG AS IT LASTS
            THE HEART THE DOG

The Angel of Despair appears while they copulate.

ANTOINE *Voice.* Who are you.

WOMAN *Voice.* I am the Angel of Despair. With my hands I dispense ecstasy, numbness, oblivion, the lust and the torment of bodies. My language is silence, my song the scream. Terror dwells in the shadows of my wings. My hope is the last gasp. My hope is the first battle. I am the knife with which the dead man cracks open his coffin. I am the one who will be. My flight is the rebellion, my sky the abyss of tomorrow.

We had arrived in Jamaica, three emissaries of the French assembly, our names Debuisson Galloudec Sasportas, our task to stir up a rebellion of the slaves against the rule of the British Crown in the name of the Republic of France. Which is the motherland of the Revolution, the terror of the thrones, the hope of the poor. Where all men are equal under the axe of Justice. Which has no bread against the hunger of its slums, but hands enough to carry the firebrand of Liberty Equality Fraternity into all countries. We stood on the square at the harbor. In the center of the square a cage had been placed. We heard the wind from the ocean, the harsh rustle of palm leaves, the bristling noise of palm fronds negro women used to sweep the dust from the square, the groaning of the slave in the cage, the surf. We saw the breasts of the negro women, the bloody welted body of the slave in the cage, the Governor's palace. We said: This is Jamaica, disgrace of the Antilles, slaveship in the Caribbean sea.

SASPORTAS Till we have done our work.

GALLOUDEC You can start right away. Didn't you come here to liberate the slaves. That in the cage is a slave. Tomorrow he will have been one if he isn't liberated today.

DEBUISSON They exhibit them in the cages when they try to run away or for other crimes, as a deterrent, till the sun withers them. It was like this when I left Jamaica, ten years ago. Don't look, Sasportas, we cannot help only one.

GALLOUDEC It's always only one who dies. The dead are the ones who are counted.

DEBUISSON Death is the mask of the Revolution.

SASPORTAS When I leave here, others will be hanging in the cages, with white skin till the sun turns them black. Then many will be better off.

GALLOUDEC Maybe we'd rather set up a guillotine. It's cleaner. The Red Widow is the best cleaning woman.

DEBUISSON The beloved of the slums.

SASPORTAS I still hold that a cage is a good thing for white skin, if the sun is high enough.

DEBUISSON We are not here to recriminate each other with the color of our skin, Citizen Sasportas.

SASPORTAS We're not equal as long as we haven't stripped each other's skin.

DEBUISSON That was a bad beginning. Let's put on our masks. I am the one I was: Debuisson, son of slaveholders in Jamaica, successor to a plantation with four hundred slaves. Returned into the womb of his family to take possession of his estate, from the clouded skies of Europe muddied by the smoke of conflagrations and the bloody stench of the new philosophy, returned to the clean air of the Caribbean after the horrors of the Revolution opened his eyes to the eternal truth that everything old is better than anything new. Besides, I am a physician, a helper of mankind without regard to status, masters or slaves, I cure the one for the other so that everything stays as it is, as long as it lasts, my face the pink face of the slaveholder who has nothing to fear in this world but death.

SASPORTAS And his slaves.

DEBUISSON Who are you, Galloudec.

GALLOUDEC A peasant from Brittany who's learned to hate the Revolution in the bloody rains of the Guillotine, I wish the rain would have poured more plentiful and not only in France, a loyal servant to his gracious lord Debuisson who believes in the holy order of monarchy and church. I hope I won't have to say this prayer too often.

DEBUISSON You've acted twice out of character, Galloudec. Who are you.

GALLOUDEC A peasant from Brittany who's learned to hate the Revolution in the bloody rains of the Guillotine. Loyal servant to his gracious lord Debuisson. I believe in the holy order of monarchy and church.

SASPORTAS *parodies.* I believe in the holy order of monarchy and church. I believe in the holy order of monarchy and church.

DEBUISSON Sasportas. Your mask.

GALLOUDEC It shouldn't be hard for you to play the slave, Sasportas, in your black skin.

SASPORTAS Fleeing from the successful black revolution in Haiti, I attached myself to Master Debuisson since God has created me for slavery. I am his slave. Is that sufficient.

Galloudec applauds.

SASPORTAS Next time I'll answer you with my knife, Citizen Galloudec.

GALLOUDEC I know your role is the most difficult to play, Sasportas. It's written all over your body.

SASPORTAS With the same whips our hands will use to write a new alphabet on other bodies.

DEBUISSON Successful revolution isn't good. You don't say that in the face of masters. Black revolution isn't good either. Blacks make a riot at best, not a revolution.

SASPORTAS Didn't the Revolution succeed in Haiti. The Black Revolution.

DEBUISSON The scum is what succeeded. The scum rules Haiti.

Sasportas spits.

DEBUISSON You're spitting in the wrong direction: I am your master. Now say it.

SASPORTAS Fleeing from the scum that turned Haiti into a cesspool.

GALLOUDEC Cesspool is good. You're learning fast, Sasportas.

DEBUISSON Take your hands off your face and look at the flesh that is dying in this cage. You too, Galloudec. It is yours and yours and my flesh. His groans are the Marseillaise of bodies the new world will be built upon. Learn the tune. We are going to hear it ever so long, like it or not, it is the tune of the Revolution, our work. Many will die in this cage before our work is done. Many will die in this cage because we do our work. That is what we do with our work for our own kind and, maybe, only that. Our place is the cage if our masks are torn before it is time. The Revolution is the mask of Death. Death is the mask of the Revolution.

A gigantic Negro enters.

DEBUISSON That is the oldest slave of my family. He is deaf and mute, a thing between man and dog. He is going to spit into the cage. Perhaps you too ought to do it, Sasportas, so you will learn to hate your black skin for as long as we need it. Then he will kiss my shoes, he is already licking his lips, you see, and on his back he will carry me, his old and new Master, into the house of my forefathers, grunting with bliss. The family opens its womb, tomorrow our work will begin.

The gigantic Negro spits into the cage, looks at Sasportas, bows before Galloudec, kisses Debuisson's shoes, carries him off on his back. Galloudec and Sasportas follow, one after the other.

THE REVOLUTION IS THE MASK OF DEATH DEATH IS THE MASK OF THE REVOLUTION THE REVOLUTION IS THE MASK OF DEATH DEATH IS THE MASK OF THE REVOLUTION THE REVOLUTION IS THE MASK OF DEATH DEATH IS THE MASK OF THE REVOLUTION THE REVOLUTION IS THE MASK OF DEATH DEATH IS THE MASK OF THE REVOLUTION THE REVOLUTION IS THE MASK OF DEATH DEATH IS THE MASK OF THE REVOLUTION THE REVOLUTION IS THE MASK OF DEATH

Return of the Prodigal Son. Father and Mother in an open cabinet. On a throne FirstLove. Debuisson Galloudec Sasportas are undressed by slaves and bedecked with costumes. Debuisson as Slaveholder, Galloudec as Overseer with his whip, Sasportas as Slave.

FIRSTLOVE Little Victor has played at Revolution. Now he comes home into the womb of his family. Home to Papa with the worm-eaten skull. Home to Mama with her smell of putrid flowers. Did you hurt yourself, little Victor. Come closer and show your wounds. Don't you know me anymore. You don't have to be afraid, little Victor. Not of me. Not of your first love. The one you have betrayed with the Revolution, you blood-smeared second love. You wallowed in the gutter with her for ten years, competing with the rabble. Or in the mortuaries where she counts her spoils. I can smell her perfume of dung. Tears, little Victor. Did you love her so much. Ah, Debuisson. I've told you she's a whore. The serpent with the bloodthirsty vulva. Slavery is a law of nature as old as mankind. Why should it end before. Look at my slaves and yours, our property. All their lives they've been animals. Why should they be humans because it is written on a piece of paper in France. Barely readable because of so much more blood than has ever been spilled for slavery here in your and my beautiful Jamaica. I'll tell you a story: In Barbados, a plantation-owner was slain two months after the abolition of slavery. His liberated slaves came to him. They walked on their knees like in church. And do you know what they wanted. To return to the protection of slavery. That is man: his first home is his mother, a prison. *Slaves lift the mother's skirts over her head in the cabinet.* Here it gapes, Home, here it yawns, the womb of the family. Just say the word if you want to go back and she will cram you into it, the idiot, the eternal Mother. The poor man in Barbados wasn't that lucky. They battered him to death with clubs, his no-more-slaves, like a rabid dog, because he didn't take them in again from the cold Spring of their Freedom beneath the beloved whip. Do you like the story, Citizen Debuisson. Liberty lives on the backs of slaves, Equality under the axe. Do you want to be my slave, little Victor. Do you love me. These are the lips that kissed you. *A female slave paints her a big mouth.* They remember your skin, Victor Debuisson. These are the breasts that warmed you, little Victor. *Female slave puts make-up on her nipples etc.* They didn't forget your mouth and your hands. This is the skin that drank your sweat. This is the womb that received your sperm which scorches my heart. *Female slave paints a blue heart on her breast.* Do you see the blue flame. Do you know how they catch runaway slaves in Cuba. They hunt them with bloodhounds. And so, Citizen Debuisson, I will take back what your whore Revolution robbed me of, my property. *Slaves as dogs chase Debuisson, accompanied by Galloudec with his whip, by the father's ghost with shouts of HUZZA.* With the fangs of my dogs I want to tear out of your soiled flesh the traces of my tears, my sweat, my cries of lust. With the knives of their claws cut out of your hide my wedding dress. I want to translate your breath that smacks of the dead bodies of kings into the language of torment that belongs to slaves. I want to eat your genitals and give birth to a tiger that will devour the time with which the clocks strike my empty heart, my heart through which the rains of the Tropics flow. *Female slave puts a tiger-mask on her face.* YESTERDAY I BEGAN / TO KILL YOU MY HEART / NOW I LOVE / YOUR CORPSE / WHEN I AM DEAD / MY DUST WILL CRY OUT FOR YOU. I want to give you this bitch for a present, little Victor, so that you can fill her with your rotten sperm. But first I want to have her flogged so that your blood will mix. Do you love me, Debuisson. One shouldn't leave a woman alone.

Slaves take the whip from Galloudec, lock the cabinet, remove the make-up from FirstLove, place Debuisson on the throne, FirstLove as a footstool, they dress up Galloudec and Sasportas as Danton and Robespierre. The Theatre of the Revolution is open. While the two players and the audience take their places, the dialogue of the parents is heard from the cabinet.

FATHER This is the resurrection of the flesh. For the worm gnaws forever and the fire won't go out. MOTHER Is he whoring around again. Crickcrack now my heart is broken, you see. FATHER I'll give her to you for a present. I'll give them both to you, black and or white. MOTHER Take the knife out of my belly. You painted whores. FATHER On your knees, bastard, and beg your Mama for her benediction. MOTHER THERE ON THE MOUNTAIN / THE WIND BLOWS WILD / THERE MARIA BUTCHERS / THE HEAVENLY CHILD. Home to Greenland. Come my children. The sun warms you there every day. FATHER Shut that babbling idiot up.

SASPORTASROBESPIERRE Go to your place, Danton, at history's pillory. Look at the parasite who devours the bread of the hungry. The libertine who rapes the daughters of the people. The traitor who turns up his nose at the smell of the blood in which the Revolution washes the body of the new society. Shall I tell you why you can't stand the look of blood anymore, Danton. Did you say Revolution. Catching hold of the fleshpots, that was your Revolution. Free passes to the brothel. That is what you strutted about for on the rostrum, applauded by the rabble. The lion who licks the aristocrat's boots. Do you savour the taste of the Bourbon's spittle. Are you warm and cozy in the asshole of the Monarchy. Did you say boldness. Go on shaking your powdered mane. You won't mock virtue much longer before your head falls under the axe of Justice. You can't say I didn't warn you, Danton. Now the guillotine, the noble invention of the new Age which will stride over you as over all traitors, is going to talk to you. Her language you'll understand, you spoke it well in September. *Slaves strike the Dantonhead off Galloudec's shoulders, chuck it to each other. Galloudec succeeds in catching it, he puts it under his arm.* Why don't you put your beautiful head between your legs, Danton, where your reason sits among the lice of your debauchery and the running sores of your depravity.

Sasportas knocks the Dantonhead from under Galloudec's arm. Galloudec crawls after the head, puts it on his shoulders.

GALLOUDECDANTON Now it's my turn. Look at the monkey with the broken jawbone. So drunk with blood he can't control his drooling. Did you bite off more than you can chew. Incorruptible one, preaching your sermon of virtue. That is the Fatherland's thanks: a policeman's fist. *Slaves rip the bandage from the jaw of Sasportas's Robespierrehead, the jawbone drops to the floor. While Sasportas searches for the bandage and the jawbone.* Did you drop something. Do you lack something. Property is theft. Do you feel the wind in your throat. That is Liberty. *Sasportas has retrieved the bandage and jawbone and restores the Robespierrehead.* Watch that your clever head doesn't get lost altogether, Robespierre, over the love of the people. Did you say Revolution. The axe of Justice, right. The guillotine is no bread factory. Thrift, thrift, Horatio. *Slaves knock the Robespierrehead off Sasportas's shoulders and use it to play soccer.* That is Equality. LONG LIVE THE REPUBLIC. Didn't I tell you: You'll be next. *Joins the soccer game of the slaves.* That is Fraternity. *SasportasRobespierre bawls.* What's wrong with soccer. Entre nous: shall I tell you why you were so keen on my beautiful head. I'll bet that when you let down your pants a cloud of dust will rise. Ladies and Gentlemen. The Theatre of the Revolution is open. Main Attraction: The Man with Half a Body. Maximilian the Great. Virtue Max. The Armchair Farter. The Masturbator from Arras. The bloody Robespierre.

SASPORTASROBESPIERRE *Puts his head on again.* My name stands forever engraved in the Pantheon of History.

GALLOUDECDANTON   A LITTLE MAN STANDS IN THE WOODS
                            MUTE WITHOUT A SOUND
                            HE WEARS A PURPLE COLORED CLOAK
                            TIGHTLY WRAPPED AROUND

SASPORTASROBESPIERRE Parasite Syphilitic Aristocrat's flunkey.

GALLOUDECDANTON Hypocrite Eunuch Lackey of Wall Street

SASPORTASROBESPIERRE Swine.

GALLOUDECDANTON Hyena.

They strike their heads from each other's shoulders. Debuisson applauds. Slaves drag him from the throne and put Sasportas on it, Galloudec as footstool. Coronation of Sasportas.

SASPORTAS The Theatre of the white Revolution is over. We sentence you to death, Victor Debuisson. Because your skin is white. Because your thoughts are white under your white skin. Because your eyes have seen the beauty of our sisters. Because your hands have touched the naked bodies of our sisters. Because your thoughts have eaten their breasts their bodies their genitals. Because you are a property owner, a master. Therefore we sentence you to death, Victor Debuisson. The snakes shall eat your shit, the crocodiles your ass, the piranhas your testicles. *Debuisson screams.* The trouble with you is that you cannot die. That's why you kill everything around you. For the sake of your dead institutions where ecstasy has no place. For the sake of your revolutions devoid of sex. Do you love this woman. We'll take her so you'll die more easily. Whoever owns nothing dies more easily. What else belongs to you. Say it quickly, our school is Time, it doesn't repeat itself and there's no breathing space for didacticism, whoever doesn't learn is going to die too. Your skin. Whom did you skin for it. Your flesh is our hunger. Your blood drains our veins. Your thoughts, right. Who sweats for your philosophies. Even your urine and your shit are exploitation and slavery. Not to mention your seed: distillate of dead bodies. Now nothing belongs to you anymore. Now you can die. Bury him.

I am standing among men who are strangers to me, in an old elevator with a metal cage that rattles during the ascent. I am dressed like an office clerk or a worker on a Sunday. I have even put on a tie, my collar rubs against my neck, I am sweating. When I move my head, the collar constricts my throat. I have been summoned to the Boss (in my thoughts I call him Number One), his office is on the fourth floor or was it the twentieth; as soon as I think about it I am not sure anymore. The message of my appointment with the Boss (whom I call Number One in my thoughts) reached me in the basement, an expansive space with empty concrete cubicles and direction signs for air raid precautions. I suppose it concerns a task that is to be assigned to me. I control the fit of my tie and fasten the knot. I would like to have a mirror so that I could also control the fit of my tie with my eyes. Impossible to ask a stranger how well your tie knot is fastened. The ties of the other men in the elevator are fastened impeccably. Some of them seem to know each other. They talk softly about something I understand nothing of. Nevertheless, their conversation must have distracted me: at the next stop I read on the indicator above the elevator doors the number eight and I am terrified. I have gone up too far or more than half the distance is still ahead of me. The time factor is crucial. FIVE MINUTES TOO EARLY WOULD BE / WHAT I'D CALL TRUE PUNCTUALITY. The last time I looked at my wrist watch the hands pointed at ten. I remember my feeling of relief: fifteen minutes remain until the hour of my appointment with the Boss. The next time I looked it was only five minutes later. As I look again at my watch, between the eighth and the ninth floor, the hands point at exactly fourteen minutes and forty-five seconds after the hour of ten: there goes my punctuality, time doesn't work to my advantage anymore. Quickly I assess my situation: at the next stop I can step out of the elevator and run down the stairway, three steps at a time, to the fourth floor. If it is the wrong floor it, of course, will mean a loss of time which probably can't be made up. I can ride on to the twentieth floor and, if the Boss's office isn't located there, ride down again to the fourth floor, provided the elevator doesn't go out of order, or I can run down the stairs (three steps at a time) and break my leg in doing so, or my neck, just because I am in a hurry. Already I can see myself lying on a stretcher which, according to my wish, will be carried into the office of the Boss where I will be placed in front of his desk, still ready though no longer fit to serve. In the meantime, everything hinges on the one question impossible to answer in advance because of my negligence: on which floor is the Boss (whom I call in my thoughts Number One) waiting for me with an important task. (It has to be an important task, why else doesn't he assign it through one of his subordinates.) A quick glance at my watch informs me irrefutably of the fact that for a long while it has been too late even for basic punctuality, though our elevator, as I notice on second glance, hasn't even arrived yet at the twelfth floor: the short hand is pointing at ten, the long hand at fifty, the seconds long since haven't mattered. Something seems to be wrong with my watch but there is no time left now for a time check: without having noticed where the other gentlemen stepped off I am alone in the elevator. With a horror that grips the roots of my hair I see on my watch which I cannot turn my eyes from any longer the hands circling the dial with increasing speed so that between two bats of an eyelid ever more hours have passed. I realize that for quite a while something has been wrong: with my watch, with the elevator, with time. I plunge into wild speculations: the force of gravity abates, a disturbance, a kind of stutter of the globe's rotation, like a cramp in the calf during a soccer game. I regret that I know too little about physics to resolve in pure science the screaming contradiction between the velocity of the elevator and the lapse of time my watch indicates. Why didn't I pay attention in school. Or read the wrong books: Poetry instead of Physics. The time is out of joint and somewhere on the

fourth or twentieth floor (the Or cuts like a knife through my negligent brain) probably in a spacious and richly carpeted room, behind his desk which probably is
placed at the far end of the room, facing the entrance, the Boss (whom in my
thoughts I call Number One) is waiting with my task for me the loser. Perhaps the
world is falling apart and my task, so important that the Boss wanted personally to
assign it to me, has already become meaningless because of my negligence, NOT
OPERATIVE in the administrative language I've learned so well (useless
knowledge!), ON FILE where no one will check anymore because the task concerned precisely the last possible action to prevent the destruction whose start I am
now experiencing, locked up in this crazed elevator with my crazed wrist watch.
Desperate dream within the dream: simply by rolling myself up into a ball, I am
able to turn my body into a bullet that by crashing through the elevator's ceiling
will outdistance time. Chilly awakening in the slow elevator to the glance at the
frantic watch. I imagine the despair of Number One. His suicide. His head—the
portrait adorns every public office—on the desk. Blood trickling from a black-
edged hole in the (probably right) temple. I didn't hear a shot but that doesn't prove anything, the walls of his office are soundproofed, of course, incidents have been
taken into account during its construction and what occurs in the Boss's office is
none of the population's business, power is lonely. I step from the elevator at the
next stop and I stand without any task on a village street in Peru, the now useless tie
still ridiculously fastened beneath my chin. Caked mud with vehicle tracks. On
both sides of the street a barren plain with occasional grass plots and patches of
gray shrubbery reaches hazily for the horizon where mountains float in the mist.
Left of the street a kind of barracks, it looks deserted, the windows black holes with
the remnants of panes. Two gigantic natives stand in front of a billboard advertis-
ing products of a foreign civilization. A menace emanates from their backs. I think
about going back, I haven't been noticed yet. Never would I have thought during
my desperate ascent to the Boss that I would feel homesick for the elevator that was
my prison. How shall I explain my presence in this no-man's-land. I don't have a
parachute to show for it, no airplane or wrecked car. Who would believe that I
came to Peru from an elevator, in front and back of me the street, flanked by the
plain which reaches for the horizon. How will communication be possible, I don't
know the language of this country, I could as well be deaf mute. I'd be better a deaf
mute: perhaps there exists compassion in Peru. The only option left to me is escape
into the space where I hope no humans dwell, maybe it's from one kind of death to
another, but I prefer hunger to the murderer's knife. In any case, I don't have the
means to buy myself off with the small amount of cash I have in foreign currency.
Destiny didn't even grant me, the employee of a deceased Boss, the favor of dying
on duty, my cause is a lost cause, my task enclosed in his brain that won't relinquish
a thing anymore this side of death until the vaults of eternity, whose combinations
the sages of the world toil to decode, are opened. Hopefully not too late, I loosen
my tie whose correct fit caused such profuse perspiration on my way to the Boss,
and let the conspicuous object vanish into my jacket. I'd almost thrown it away, a
clue. Turning around, I see the village for the first time; mud and straw, through
an open door a hammock. Cold sweat at the thought I could have been watched
from inside but I can't discover any sign of life, the only movement a dog rummag-
ing in a smoldering pile of garbage. I've hesitated too long: the men turn away

from the billboard and, diagonally crossing the street, walk in my direction, at first without looking at me. I see their faces hovering over me, one of them blurred and black, the eyes white, impossible to figure out their look: the eyes are without pupils. The other one's head is of gray silver. A long quiet look from eyes whose color I can't determine, there is a red gleam in them. A twitching moves through the fingers of the heavy dangling right hand which seems also to be of silver, the blood vessels shining through the metal. The silver man passes behind me following the black one. My fear subsides and makes room for disappointment: I am not even worth a knife or the stranglehold of metal hands. The quiet look, directed at me for five steps, didn't it betray something like contempt. What is my crime. The world hasn't been destroyed, provided that this isn't another world. How do you accomplish an unknown task. What could my task be in this wasteland on the other side of civilization. How is the employee supposed to know what's going on in the head of the Boss. No science in this world is going to drag my lost task from the brain tissue of the deceased. It will be buried with him, the state funeral which probably is taking place this very moment, doesn't warrant the resurrection. Something like serenity grows within me, I sling my jacket over my shoulder and unbutton the collar of my shirt: my walk has become a stroll. In front of me, the dog runs across the street carrying a hand sideways in his muzzle, the fingers point in my direction, they looked charred. Some young men cross my way with a menacing remark that isn't meant for me. Where the street recedes into the plain a woman stands poised as if she has been waiting for me. I stretch my arms out for her, how long since they've touched a woman, and I hear a male voice say THIS WOMAN IS THE WIFE OF A MAN. It sounds final and I keep walking. When I look back the woman stretches her arms out for me and bares her breasts. On a railway embankment overgrown with grass, two boys are tinkering with a hybrid of a steam engine and a locomotive that stands on a broken track. As a European I see at first glance that their labor is wasted: this vehicle is never going to move, but I don't tell the children, to work is to hope, and I keep walking into the landscape that has no other work but to wait for the disappearance of man. Now I know my destination. I cast off my clothes, outward appearances don't matter anymore. Eventually THE OTHER ONE, the antipode, the doppelgänger, will meet me, he with my face of snow. One of us will survive.

Debuisson. Galloudec. Sasportas.

DEBUISSON *hands Galloudec a piece of paper. Galloudec and Sasportas read.* The government which gave us the task to organize a rebellion of the slaves here in Jamaica isn't in office anymore. The General Bonaparte has dissolved the Directorate with the bayonets of his grenadiers. France is called Napoleon. The world will be what it was, a home for masters and slaves. *Galloudec crumbles the paper.* What are you gaping at. Our company has been struck from the commercial register. It is bankrupt. The merchandise we are offering for sale, payable in the standard currency TearsSweatBlood, isn't traded anymore in this world. *Tears the paper.* I free us of our task. You, Galloudec, the peasant from Brittany. You, Sasportas, the son of slavery. Me, Debuisson.

SASPORTAS *softly.* The son of slaveholders.

DEBUISSON Each to his own freedom or slavery. Our play is over, Sasportas. Watch out when you take off your make-up, Galloudec. Maybe your skin will come off with it. Your mask, Sasportas, is your face. My face is my mask. *Covers his face with his hands.*

GALLOUDEC This is going too fast for me, Debuisson. I am a peasant, I can't think that fast. I have risked my neck for a year and more now, preached till my tongue was shredded during secret meetings, smuggled arms through cordons of bloodhounds, sharks, and informers, as your dog acted the idiot at the supper tables of British cutthroats, scorched by the sun and convulsed by fever on this godforsaken continent without snow, and all that for this lazy mass of black flesh that won't move except when kicked by the boot, and what business of mine is the slavery in Jamaica, anyway, I'm a Frenchman after all—Wait, Sasportas—but I want to turn black on the spot if I understand why all that shouldn't be true anymore and cancelled and no task for nothing anymore, because in Paris a general is getting cocky. He isn't even a Frenchman. But if someone listened to your talk, Debuisson, he would believe you were just waiting for this General Bonaparte.

DEBUISSON Maybe I did wait for this General Bonaparte. The same way that half of France waited for him. Revolution is a tiring business, Galloudec. When nations sleep, generals rise and smash the yoke of freedom which is such a heavy burden. Do you feel how it misshapes your shoulders, Galloudec.

SASPORTAS I believe I don't understand you either, Debuisson. Not anymore. The world a home for masters and slaves. Slaves have no home, Citizen Debuisson. And as long as there are masters and slaves, we won't be released from our task. What's a general's coup in Paris got to do with our task, the liberation of slaves in Jamaica. Ten thousand men wait for our command, for yours if you like. But it need not be your voice that speaks the command. They're not asleep, they're not waiting for a general. They're ready to kill and to die for your YOKE OF FREEDOM they've been dreaming of us as of an unknown love, all their lives which are a daily death. They don't ask about the shape of her breasts or the virginity of her womb. What is Paris to these men, a distant stone pile that was for a short time the metropolis of their hope; what's France to them, a country where the sun can't kill, where for a short time blood had the color of dawn, somewhere on a pale-faced continent on the other side of the grave of Atlantis. Your general, I have already forgotten his name, nobody will talk of him anymore when the name of Haiti's liberator is printed in every school book.

Debuisson laughs.

SASPORTAS You're laughing.

DEBUISSON I'm laughing, Sasportas, ask me why.

SASPORTAS Maybe, again I didn't understand you. I don't know if I should kill you now or if I should apologize.

DEBUISSON Do as you like, Sasportas.

SASPORTAS *laughs.* Ah, Debuisson. For one moment I believed what you're saying is your true opinion. I ought to have known better. I ought to have known it was a test. I didn't pass the test, did I. Each one of us must be cold as a knife when the signal is given and the battle is about to begin. It isn't fear that makes my nerves tremble but the anticipation of the dance. I hear the drums before they are beaten. I hear with my pores, my skin is black. But I doubted you, and that isn't good. Forgive me, Debuisson. You steeped your hands in blood for our cause. I saw that it wasn't easy for you. I love you for both, Debuisson, because the man who had to be killed so he couldn't betray our cause was of my own kind, and he needed his death before the next torture. As a physician and a helper of mankind you were supposed to cure him of the results of the previous one, but he said: Kill me so I cannot betray, and you killed him for our cause, as a physician and a revolutionary. *Sasportas embraces Debuisson.*

DEBUISSON You needn't apologize, Sasportas, it was not a test. Our names won't be printed in the school books and your liberator of Haiti where now the liberated negroes are knocking the liberated mulattoes, or vice versa, will wait a long time for his place in the Book of History. In the meantime, Napoleon will change France into a barracks and Europe probably into a battlefield, commerce will thrive in any case, and peace with England won't fail to come, what unifies mankind but business. The Revolution has no home anymore, that isn't news under this sun which probably will never shine upon a new earth, slavery has many faces, we haven't seen its last one yet, not you, Sasportas, and neither have we, Galloudec, and what we believed to be the dawn of freedom was maybe only the mask of a new, even more hideous slavery compared to which the rule of the whip on the Caribbean islands and elsewhere represents merely a friendly foretaste of the pleasures of Paradise and your unknown love, freedom, when all her masks are exhausted, has probably no other face after all but treason: what you won't betray today, will kill you tomorrow. From the viewpoint of Human Medicine the Revolution is stillborn, Sasportas: from the Bastille to the Conciergerie, the liberator turns into the jailer. DEATH TO THE LIBERATORS is the final truth of the Revolution. And as for my murder in the service of our cause: the physician-as-murderer isn't a new part in the theatre of society, death doesn't mean that much to the helpers of mankind: a different chemical condition, until the final triumph of the desert each ruin is a construction site resisting the fangs of time. Perhaps I only washed my hands, Sasportas, when I was steeping them in blood for our cause, poetry was always the language of no avail, my black friend. We're carrying other corpses on our back now, and they will kill us if we don't throw them off before we hit the pit. Your death is called Liberty, Sasportas, your death is called Fraternity, Galloudec, my death is called Equality. They were good to ride when they were still our nags, the winds of Tomorrow brushing our temple. Now the wind is blowing from Yesterday. The nags, that's us. Do you feel the spurs in your flesh. Our riders have their baggage: the dead victims of terror, pyramids of death. Do you feel the weight. They're getting heavier with every doubt that creeps through the ganglia of our brain. A revolution has no time to count its dead. And we need our time now to call off the black revolution we prepared so thoroughly in the name of a future that already has become the past like the others before it. Why is it that the future is only singular in our language, Galloudec. Among the dead it's probably different if the dust has a voice. Think about it, Sasportas, before you risk your neck for the liberation of the slaves into an abyss that has no bottom anymore since the arrival of this message which I am going to swallow now so there won't be any trace left of our work. Do you too want a scrap. That was our task, it tastes of nothing but paper now. Tomorrow it will have gone the way of all flesh, every ascension has a direction, and perhaps the star is already on its way from the cold of outer space, a lump of ice or metal, that will knock the terminal hole into the pro- verbial bottom of facts where we keep planting our feeble hopes again and again. Or the cold itself which will freeze our yesterdays and our tomorrows into an eter- nal today. Why aren't we born as trees, Sasportas, to them all this is of no concern. Or would you rather be a mountain. Or a desert. What do you say, Galloudec. Why are you gaping at me like two stones. Why can't we simply exist and watch the war of the landscapes. What do you want of me. Die your own death if life isn't to your taste. I won't help you into the grave, life isn't to my taste either. Yesterday I dreamed I was walking through New York. The neighborhood was dilapidated and uninhabited by whites. On the sidewalk in front of me, a golden serpent rose up and when I crossed the street or rather the jungle of seething metal that was the street, another serpent arose on the other sidewalk. It was a radiant blue. I knew in my dream: the golden serpent is Asia, the blue serpent, that is Africa. When I woke up I forgot it again. We are three worlds. Why do I know it now. And I heard a voice say: AND BEHOLD THERE WAS A GREAT EARTHQUAKE FOR THE ANGEL OF THE LORD DESCENDED FROM THE HEAVEN AND CAME AND ROLLED BACK THE STONE FROM THE DOOR AND SAT UPON IT AND HIS COUNTENANCE WAS LIKE LIGHTNING AND HIS RAIMENTS WHITE AS SNOW. I don't want to know all that anymore. For a thousand years our three loves have been laughed at. They have wallowed in all the gutters, they have swum down all the sewers of this world, they have been dragged through all the brothels, our whore Liberty, our whore Equality, our whore Fraternity. Now I want to sit where they laugh, free to do anything that's to my taste, equal to myself, my own and no one else's brother. Your hide will stay black, Sasportas. You, Galloudec, will remain a peasant. You're laughed at. My place is where they laugh at you. I laugh at you. I laugh at the nigger. I laugh at the peasant. I laugh at the nigger who wants to wash himself white with Liberty. I laugh at the peasant who struts about in the mask of Equality. I laugh at the stupidity of Fraternity that made me, Debuisson, master of four hundred slaves—I only need to say Yes, Yes and Yes to the sacred institution of slavery—that stupidity which made me blind to your dirty slave's hide, Sasportas, to your four-legged peasant's trot, Galloudec, on your neck the yoke the oxen walk under in the furrow of your field that doesn't even belong to you. I want my piece of the cake of the world. I will cut myself my piece from the hunger of the world. You, you don't own a knife.

SASPORTAS You've torn up a flag I believed in. I want to cut myself a new one from my black hide. *Cuts with the knife a cross into his palm.* That's the farewell, Citizen Debuisson. *Presses his bleeding hand on Debuisson's face.* Do you enjoy the taste of my blood. I've said that slaves have no home. That isn't true. The home of slaves is the rebellion. I will enter the battle armed with the humiliations of my life. You have handed me a new weapon and I thank you for it. Could be my place is at the gallows and perhaps a rope is growing around my neck while I talk to you rather than kill you, to whom I owe nothing now but my knife. But death is of no importance and at the gallows I will know that my accomplices are the negroes of all races whose number grows with every minute you spend at your slaveholder's trough or between the legs of your white whore. When the living can no longer fight, the dead will. With every heartbeat of the revolution flesh grows back on their bones, blood in their veins, life in their death. The rebellion of the dead will be the war of the landscapes, our weapons the forests, the mountains, the oceans, the deserts of the world. I will be forest, mountain, ocean, desert. I—that is Africa. I—that is Asia. The two Americas—that is I.

GALLOUDEC I will go with you, Sasportas. All of us must die, Debuisson. And that's the only thing we still have in common. After the massacre in Guadeloupe, they found in the midst of a pile of corpses, all of them black, one white man who was just as dead. However, that can't happen to you anymore, Debuisson. You are out of this.

DEBUISSON Stay. I am afraid, Galloudec, of the beauty of the world. I know very well it is the mask of treason. Don't leave me alone with my mask, it is growing already into my flesh and doesn't hurt anymore. Kill me before I betray you. I am afraid, Sasportas, of the shame to be happy in this world.

Said whispered screamed Debuisson. But Galloudec and Sasportas went away, one with the other, leaving Debuisson alone with Treason who had come up to him like the serpent from the stone. Debuisson closed his eyes against the temptation to look at the face of his first love who was Treason. Treason danced. Debuisson pressed his hands against his eyes. He heard his heart beating the rhythm of the dance steps. They grew faster with his heartbeat. Debuisson felt his eyelids twitching against his palms. Perhaps the dance had already ended and only his heart was still booming while Treason, her arms crossed perhaps over her breasts, or her hands placed on her hips or, by this time, grabbing her crotch, her vulva probably quivering already with lust, looked with swimming eyes at him, Debuisson, who just now was pushing his eyes into their sockets with his fists, afraid of his hunger for the shame of happiness. Maybe Treason had left him already. His own greedy hands failed Debuisson. He opened his eyes. Treason smiling showed her breasts and silently spread her legs wide open, her beauty hit Debuisson like an axe. He forgot the storm of the Bastille, the Hungermarch of the Eighty-thousand, the end of the Gironde, their Last Supper, a corpse at the banquet, Saint Just, the Black Angel, Danton, the Voice of the Revolution, Marat hunched over the dagger, Robespierre's broken jaw, his scream when the executioner ripped off the bandage, his last pitying look at the exultant mob. Debuisson clutched at the last memory that hadn't left him yet: a sandstorm off the coast of Las Palmas, crickets were blown with the sand unto the ship and stayed for the passage across the Atlantic. Debuisson ducked against the sandstorm, rubbed the sand from his eyes, covered his ears against the song of the crickets. Then Treason threw herself upon him like a heaven, the bliss of the labia a dawn.

END

Quartet

edited by W. Storch, Frankfurt/Main 1980: "Artaud, the language of pain. Writing from the experience that the masterworks are the accomplices of power. Thinking at the end of Enlightenment, thinking that begun with the death of God; Enlightenment the coffin He was buried in, and it is putrefying with His corpse. Life imprisoned in this coffin. 'Thinking is one of the greatest joys of mankind'—Brecht has Galileo say this before the instruments of torture are shown to him. The lightning that split Artaud's consciousness was Nietzsche's experience that thinking might be the last joy of mankind. Artaud is the terminal case. He wrested literature from the hands of the police, the theatre from the hands of medicine. His texts blossom under the sun of torture that is shining with equal force on all continents of this planet. Read on the ruins of Europe, his texts will be classics."

C.W.

CHARACTERS

MERTEUIL
VALMONT

TIMESPACE

Drawing room before the French revolution.
Air raid shelter after World War III.

MERTEUIL Valmont. I believed your passion for me died. Why this sudden fire again? And with such youthful force. However, it's too late. You won't ignite my heart anymore. Not once again. Never more. I am telling you this not without regret, Valmont. After all, there were minutes—maybe, I should say moments, a minute that is an eternity—when I was happy thanks to your company. I am talking of myself, Valmont. What do I know of your feelings. And I should perhaps talk rather about the minutes during which I could use you—you, that was your talent in the intercourse with my physiology—to feel something that in my memory seems to be a sensation of bliss. You didn't forget how to manipulate this engine. Don't take your hand away. It's not that I am feeling anything for you. It is my skin that remembers. Or perhaps it doesn't matter to it—I am talking of my skin, Valmont—simply doesn't matter, does it? to what kind of animal the instrument of its lust is attached, hand or claw. When I close my eyes you are beautiful, Valmont. Or hunchbacked if I want it. The privilege of the blind. They drew the better lot in love. They are spared the comedy of circumstances: they see what they want to see. The ideal would be blind and deafmute. The love of stones. Did I shock you, Valmont. How easy it is to discourage you. I didn't know you like this. Did the fair sex wound you deeply after me. Tears. Do you have a heart, Valmont. Since when. Or was your virility damaged in my successors. Your breath tastes of solitude. Did the successor of my successor send you packing. The forsaken lover. No. Don't retract your tender offer, Sir. I am buying. I am buying in any case. No need to fear emotions. Why should I hate you, I didn't love you. Let's rub our hides together. Ah, the bondage of bodies. The agony to live and not be God. To have a consciousness but no power over matter. Do not rush, Valmont. That is good. Yes yes yes yes. That was well acted, wasn't it. What do I care for the lust of my body, I am no dairy-maid. My brain is working at its normal rate. I am totally cold, Valmont. My life My death My love.

Enter Valmont.

MERTEUIL Valmont. You are coming exactly on the minute. And I almost regret your punctuality. It's cutting short a bliss I'd have loved to share with you, wouldn't it be based on its indivisibility alone if you understand what I mean.

VALMONT Do I understand you if I assume that you are in love again, Marchioness. Well, I am too if you want to call it that. Once again. I would be sorry should I have prevented a lover's attack on your beautiful person. Through which window did he climb out. May I hope he has broken his neck in doing so.

MERTEUIL Fie, Valmont. And save your compliments for the lady of your heart wherever this organ might be located. I hope for your sake its new sheath is gilded. You ought to know me better. In love. I thought we agreed that what you call love belongs to the realm of servants. How can you consider me capable of such a vulgar stirring. The greatest bliss is the bliss of animals. Rarely enough it drops into our lap. You let me feel it once in a while when I still liked to use you for it, Valmont, and I hope you didn't leave empty handed either. Who is the lucky one of the moment. Or may we already call her the unlucky one.

VALMONT It is La Tourvel. As for your indivisible

MERTEUIL Jealous. You, Valmont. What a regression. I could understand you if you would know him. By the way, I am certain you have met him. An attractive man. Though he looks like you. Even birds migrating flutter in the nets of habit though their flight spans the continents. Turn around once. His advantage is his youth. In bed as well if you want to know. Do you want to know. A dream if I assume you are reality, Valmont, begging your pardon. In ten years perhaps there won't be any difference between you if I could turn you into a stone now with one loving glance of the Medusa. Or into a more pleasing substance. A fertile notion: the museum of our loves. We would have full houses, wouldn't we, Valmont, with the statues of our putrefied desires. Those dead dreams classified according to the alphabet or lined up in chronological order, free of the accidents of the flesh, not exposed anymore to the horrors of change. Our memory needs those crutches: one doesn't even remember the various bends of cocks, not to mention faces: a haze. La Tourvel is an insult. I didn't release you into liberty so you could mount this cow, Valmont. I could understand it if you would take an interest in little Volange, a vegetable fresh from a convent's discipline, my virginal niece, but La Tourvel. I admit she is a mighty piece of flesh but to be shared with a husband who has sunk his teeth into it, a loyal husband as I have good reason to fear, and for who knows how many years. What's left for you, Valmont. The dregs. Do you seriously want to poke around in those muddy leftovers. I pity you, Valmont. If she were a whore who had learned her trade. La Merreaux, for example, I would share her with ten men. But the only lady of high society perverse enough to enjoy herself in wedlock, a bigot with reddened knees from the pew and swollen fingers from wringing her hands before her father confessor. Those hands won't touch a genital, Valmont, without the blessing of the church. I'll bet she is dreaming of immaculate concep-tion when her loving spouse lowers himself on her with the conjugal intention to make her a child, once every year. What is the devastation of a landscape compared to the despoiling of lust through the loyalty of a husband. Of course, the Count Gercourt contemplates the innocence of my niece. In good faith, by the way; the bill of sale is filed with the magistrate. And perhaps you are afraid of his competition, he already snatched La Vressac from under your nose, and you were two years younger at the time. You are getting old, Valmont. I thought it would be a pleasure for you, besides a ride on the virgin, to crown the beautiful animal Gercourt with the inevitable antlers before he assumes the gamekeeper's office, and all the poachers of the capital raid his forest and keep renewing his subscription for this headgear. Be a good dog, Valmont, and pick up the scent as long as it is fresh. A little youth in your bed since the mirror doesn't provide it anymore. Why lift your leg at a poor box. Or are you pining for the alms of marriage. Shall we give an example to the world and marry each other, Valmont.

VALMONT How could I dare insult you thus, Marchioness, in front of all the world. The alms could be poisoned. By the way, I prefer to select my hunt myself. Or the tree I am lifting my leg at, as you like to call it. Rain hasn't fallen on you in a long time, when did you last look in the mirror, friend of my soul. I wish I could still serve you as a cloud but the wind is driving me towards new skies. I don't doubt I will make the poor box blossom. As for the competition: Marchioness, I know your long memory. You won't forget even in hell that the president preferred Tourvel to you. I am prepared to become the loving tool of your revenge. And I expect a better hunt from the object of my adoration than from your virginal niece, unexperienced as she is in the arts of fortification. What could she have learned in the convent but fasting and a little Godpleasing masturbation with the crucifix. I bet that after the frost of filial prayers she burns for the coup de grace to put an end to her innocence. She will run into my knife before I have even drawn it. She won't even double once: she doesn't know the thrills of the hunt. What is game to me without the lust of the chase. Without the sweat of fear, the choked breath, the turning upward of the white in the eye. What's left is digestion. My best tricks will make a fool of me like the empty theatre does of the actor. I will have to applaud myself. The tiger as a ham. Let the rabble fornicate between door and threshold, their time is expensive, it's costing us money; our noble vocation is to kill time. It demands everything of a human being; there is too much of it. Happy he who could make the clocks of the world stand still: eternity as an eternal erection. Time is the void of creation, all of mankind fits into it. For the rabble, the church has stuffed it with God, we know it is black and has no bottom. If the rabble is going to find this out, they'll stuff us into it after Him.

MERTEUIL The clocks of the world. Do you have difficulty, Valmont, to make your better self stand erect.

VALMONT With you, Marchioness. Though I do have to admit that I am beginning to understand why loyalty is the wildest of all debaucheries. Too late as far as our tender relation is concerned, but I am planning to exercise this new experience a bit. I hate times past. Change accumulates them. Look at our nails, we go on sprouting in the coffin. And imagine if we had to dwell among the refuse of our years. Pyramids of filth, until the tape rips at the finish line. Or in the secretions of our bodies. Death alone is eternal, life keeps repeating itself until the abyss yawns. The deluge is a deficiency of canalization. As for the loving husband: he is in a foreign country on some secret mission. Maybe he'll succeed, political animal that he is, in starting some war or other. An effective poison against the boredom of devastation. Life moves faster when dying becomes a stage play, the beauty of the world cuts less deeply into the heart—do we have a heart, Marchioness—as we watch its destruction; you're watching the parade of young buttocks which confronts us day in, day out, with our own mortality—we can't have all of them, can we, and the clap to each one who managed to escape us!—you're watching them in front of sword points and in the flash of cannon fire with some composure. Do you sometimes think of death, Marchioness. What is your mirror telling you. It is always the other one who looks back. It is him we search for when we burrow through unknown bodies, away from ourselves. Maybe, neither one nor the other exists, only the void in our soul that crows for its fill. When are you going to put your virginal niece on view, Marchioness.

MERTEUIL Did you find the way back into your own hide, Valmont. There is no man whose member won't stiffen at the thought of his dear flesh departing, fear makes philosophers. Welcome to sin and forget the poor box before piety overpowers you and you forget your one true vocation. What else have you learned but to maneuver your cock into a cunt resembling the one you once fell out of, always with the same more or less pleasant result, and always deluded that the applause of those alien mucous membranes is meant for you, and only you, that those screams of lust are addressed to you, while you are nothing but a barren vehicle, indifferent and totally interchangeable, for the lust of the woman who is using you, the power drunk fool of her creation. You know well enough that every man is one man too few for a woman. You also know, Valmont: soon enough fate will catch up with you and you won't even be that anymore, a man too few. Even the gravedigger will enjoy himself with us.

VALMONT I am bored with the bestiality of our conversation. Every word rips a gash, every smile bares a fang. We should let tigers play our parts. Another bite, please, another strike of the paw. The stage craft of wild beasts.

MERTEUIL You are going to pieces, Valmont, you're becoming sentimental. Virtue is an infectious disease. What is that thing, our soul. A muscle or mucous membrane. What I am afraid of is the night of the bodies. Four days journey from Paris in a mudhole that belongs to my family, that chain of members and wombs threaded on the string of an accidental name bestowed on an unwashed ancestor by a stinking king, there something lives—half human, half cattle. I hope I will never see it in this life, or in another life if there is another life. The mere thought of its stench makes me sweat from all my pores. My mirrors are oozing its blood. It doesn't cloud my image, I laugh about the sufferings of others like any animal gifted with reason. But sometimes I dream that it is stepping out of my mirrors on its feet of dung and without any kind of face, but I see its hands clearly, claws and hoofs, when it rips the silk off my thighs and throws itself on top of me like soil on a coffin, and maybe its violence is the key that unlocks my heart. Go now, Valmont. The virgin tomorrow night at the opera.

Exit Valmont.

MERTEUIL Madame Tourvel. My heart at your feet. Don't be shocked, beloved of my soul. Can you believe that a lecherous thought dwells in this breast after so many weeks of your pious company. I admit I was a different man before the lightning flash of your eyes struck me. Valmont the breaker of hearts. I AM BREAKING THE HEARTS OF THE PROUDEST OF WOMEN. I didn't know you, Madame. Shame even to think of it. What filth I have waded through. What art of dissembling. What depravity. Sins like scarlet fever. The mere glimpse of a beautiful woman—what am I saying?—of a fishwife's behind, and I turned into a beast of prey. I was an abyss, Madame. Would you like to venture a look into it—I wanted to say downwards, forgive me—from the height of your virtue. I see you blush. How does this red come to your cheeks, my love. It suits you. But where does your imagination get these colors to paint for you my vices. From the sacrament of matrimony, perhaps, which I believed armored you against the worldly forces of seduction. I would be tempted to display for you my sins down to the smallest detail—are you eager for my catalogue—if only to see your becoming blush a bit longer. At least it gives some evidence that there is blood pulsing in your veins. Blood. The cruel fate not to be the first one. Don't make me think of it. And even if you would open your veins for me, all your blood could not compensate for the wedding another man took away from me, forever. The moment never to be recovered. The deadly "once and never again" of the batting eyelid. Andsoforth. Don't make me think of it. Don't be afraid. I respect the sacred bond that joins you to your spouse, and should he not find the way into your bed anymore I'd be the first to help him on top. His lust is my joy since your virtue has taught me to hate the rake I used to be, and I know your womb is sealed. I hardly dare kiss your hand. And if I make so bold it is not worldly passion that drives me on. Don't take away your hand, Madame. A drink in the desert. Even the love of God needs a body. Why else did He let his son become human and give him the cross for a lover. THE FLESH HAS ITS OWN SPIRIT. Do you want to be my cross. You are already by virtue of the sacrament of your marriage to another but me. But maybe your body has one or another secret entrance that is not covered by this interdiction, one forgotten or scorned by the love of Monsieur Le President. Can you believe that so much beauty should have the sole purpose of reproduction and only one eternal center. Isn't it blasphemy to reserve this mouth to the in and out of breathing, to the drudgery of absorbing food, and the golden middle of this magnificent behind to the sad labor of discharging excrement. Can this tongue move only syllables and dead matter. What a waste. And what avarice at the same time. Twins of vices. Yes, you blaspheme, Madame, if you leave the wear and tear of your gifts to the ravages of time and to the tender fauna of the graveyard. Can it be less than a mortal sin not to do what we have been blessed to think. To strangle the offspring of our blessed brains before their first timid cry. This instrument of our bodies, isn't it given to us so it may be played upon until silence breaks the strings. The thought that doesn't become deed poisons the soul. To live with the mortal sin of discrimination and refusal. To die only partly used. The salvation of your mortal soul is what's at my heart, Madame, during each attempt at your unfortunately perishable body. You will leave it behind more easily when it's been fully used. Heaven is covetous of all matter and hell is scrupulous, it punishes idleness and neglect, its eternal tortures prefer the neglected parts. The deepest fall into hell is from the heights of innocence.

Enter Valmont.

VALMONT I shall think about it, my dear Valmont. It moves me to see you so worried about the salvation of my soul. I won't forget to tell my husband that heaven appointed him the regent of all my orifices. Not without mentioning the unselfish source from which this revelation sprang at me. I see you share my joyous anticipation of the voyages of discovery in the matrimonial bed. You are a saint, Valmont. Or should I have deceived myself about you. Should you have deceived me. Are you playing a game with me. What is this grimace hiding. A mask or a face. The horrible suspicion is growing in my heart that you drape a very worldly passion with the cloak of piety. Fear, Valmont, the wrath of an insulted wife.

MERTEUIL Fear. What should I fear from your wrath but the restoration of my shaken virtue. Fear. What is the conversion of the sinner without the dagger's daily stab of lust, the sting of remorse, the benefit of chastisement. Fear. I am asking for your wrath, Madame. Like the desert for the rain, like the blind man for the lightning which explodes the night of his eyes. Do not withhold your punishing hand from my unruly flesh. Every blow will be a caress, every gash from your nails a gift of heaven, every bite a monument.

VALMONT I am no goose, Valmont, as you would like to believe. I won't give you the pleasure of being a tool of your degenerate lust. Tears, My lord.

MERTEUIL What else, Queen. You kill me when you talk daggers. Spill my blood if that will soothe your wrath. But don't mock my noblest sentiments. This frivolity doesn't rise from your beautiful soul. You shouldn't copy a monster like La Merteuil. You are a bad copy, it does you credit. Forgive me if I moisten your hand, only you are able to stop the flow of my tears. Let me rest in your lap—ah, you still don't trust me. Let me dispel your doubts. A trial of my constancy. For example, bare these breasts, the armor of your dress cannot conceal their beauty anyway. Lightning shall strike me if I even lift my eyes. Not to mention my hand, it shall wither away if

VALMONT Fall, Valmont. Fall, lightning did strike you. And take your hand away, it has a putrid smell.

MERTEUIL You are cruel.

VALMONT I?

MERTEUIL By the way, I have to make a confession. You are taking upon yourself a deadly offence by defending your conjugal bed.

VALMONT So you'll die for a good cause and we shall meet again before the face of God.

MERTEUIL I am not familiar with the geography of the heavens. I'd be mortified to miss you in the Elysian fields which are densely populated if we are to believe the church. But I am not talking of myself: at issue is the blood of a virgin. The niece of the monster, the little Volange. She is pursuing me. Church, drawing room or playhouse, as soon as she sees me from afar, she waves her virginal behind towards my weak flesh. A vessel of evil, the more dangerous because it is completely innocent, a roseate tool of hell, a menace from the void. Ah, this void within me. It is growing and will swallow me. Daily it demands sacrifice. One day temptation will engulf me. I shall be the devil who thrusts this child into eternal damnation, if you do not offer me your hand and more, you my guardian angel who carries me across the abyss on the wings of love. Do it, make this sacrifice for the sake of your helpless sister, since you are afraid of the flame which burns me to ashes and keep your heart cold for me. After all, there is less at stake for you than for a virgin. Do I have to tell you what heaven thinks of this. Hell will thank you threefold if you keep insisting on your undivided bed. Your coldness, Madame, is throwing three souls into the eternal flames, and what is a murder compared to the crime against even one soul.

VALMONT Do I understand you correctly, Vicomte. Because you are unable to bridle your lechery or, how did you call it, the growing void within you to which you have to sacrifice every day—isn't your philosophical vacuum rather the daily need of your very worldly sexual duct?—and because this one virgin didn't learn to move with propriety—what debauched convent must she have grown up in—the happiness of my marriage shall be

MERTEUIL That is not you. This cold heart is not yours. You save or condemn three immortal souls, Madame, by pledging or withholding a body that will pass away in any case. Think of your better self. The pleasure will be multiple: the end sanctifies the means, the sting of the sacrifice will make the happiness of your marriage even more complete.

VALMONT You know I'd rather kill myself than

MERTEUIL And renounce bliss. I am talking of the eternal kind.

VALMONT It is enough, Valmont.

MERTEUIL Yes, it is enough. Forgive the terrible trial I had to subject you to so I could learn what I know: Madame, you are an angel and my price is not too high.

VALMONT Which price, my friend.

MERTEUIL The lifelong renunciation of the arousal of lust which filled my other life to the brim, ah, how far behind me it is now for lack of a subject worthy of my adoration. Let me at your feet

VALMONT The devil knows many disguises. A new mask, Valmont?

MERTEUIL See the evidence of my truth. By what means should I become dangerous to you, with what penetrate into the crypt of your virtue. The devil has no part of me anymore, worldly lust no weapon. WASTE AND VOID THE SEA IS QUIET. If you won't believe your eyes convince yourself with your tender hand. Put your hand, Madame, on the empty spot between my thighs. Don't be afraid of anything, I am all soul. Your hand, Madame.

VALMONT You are a saint, Valmont. I permit you to kiss my feet.

MERTEUIL You make me happy, Madame. And throw me back into my abyss. Tonight at the opera, I shall again be exposed to the lures of that certain virgin the devil has recruited against me. Should I avoid her. Virtue becomes lazy without toiling at the thorn of temptation. Wouldn't you despise me if I shunned the danger. MAN MUST VENTURE INTO THE HOSTILE WORLD. Every art needs to be exercised. Don't send me unarmed into battle. Three souls will be in the eternal fire if this my barely tamed flesh sprouts anew before the young blossom. The prey has its power over the hunter, sweet are the terrors of the opera. Let me measure my small strength against your naked beauty, Queen, protected as you are by the fence of matrimony, so I can hold up your sacred image in front of my eyes when I, confined in my weak flesh, have to step out into the dark arena to face the spearheads of maiden breasts.

VALMONT I ask myself if you will resist those breasts, Vicomte. I see you wavering. Should we have deceived ourselves about the degree of your sanctity. Will you endure the tougher test. Here it is. I am a woman, Valmont. Can you look at a woman and not be a man.

MERTEUIL I can, Lady. As you see, your offer makes no muscle twitch, no nerve quiver inside me. I scorn you with a light heart, share my joy. Tears. You are crying with good reason, Queen. Tears of joy, I know it. With good reason you are proud to have been so scorned. I see you have understood me. Cover yourself, my love. An unchaste draught could brush you, cold as a husband's hand.

Pause.

VALMONT I believe I could get used to being a woman, Marchioness.

MERTEUIL I wish I could.

Pause.

VALMONT What now. Are we to go on playing.

MERTEUIL Are we playing? Go on to what?

VALMONT Adored virgin, beautiful child, most charming niece. Ah, the sight of your innocence makes me forget my sex and changes me into your aunt who commended you so warmly to me. Not an edifying thought. I shall bore myself to death in her sorry impersonation. I know every spot on her soul. I shall say nothing of the rest. But the doom between my legs—pray with me that it won't overcome you in its rebellion against my virtue, and close the abyss of your eyes before it devours us—makes me nearly wish for the exchange. Yes, I wish I could exchange it, this my sex, here in the shadow of the danger of losing myself completely to your beauty. A loss only to be made up by the destruction of the portrait in the ecstasy of lust it so urgently invites. Lust alone takes the blindfold from love's eyes and grants them the view through the veil of the skin to the coarseness of the flesh, the indifferent food of graves. God must have wanted it, what. Why else the weapon called face. Whoever creates wants the destruction. And not until the flesh rots away has the soul time off. Better you shed it immediately. If you were ugly. Only the timely liberation from the attributes of beauty is insurance against the Fall. And that won't suffice, everything or nothing, nothing can happen to a skeleton except the wind playing with the bones on the other side of sin. Let us forget what stands between us before it unites us for the duration of one spasm—am I doing well, Marchioness—we all do our gymnastics at the umbilical cord, and permit me to offer you my male protection, the strong arm of a father, against the malice of the world the silence of your convent didn't acquaint you with. I know, believe me, my ominous sex, and the thought splits my heart that a worthless brute, dull novice, lewd farmhand could break that seal with which nature protects the secret of your virginal womb. I'd rather fall into sin myself than suffer such injustice that cries to high heaven.

MERTEUIL Does it cry. What is that fatherly hand, Monsieur, searching for those parts of my body the Mother Superior forbade me to touch.

VALMONT Why father. Let me be your priest, who is more a father than the priest who opens the gates of paradise for all of God's children. The key is in my hand, the signpost, the heavenly tool, the fiery sword. The matter is urgent: before the niece becomes the aunt the lesson has to be learned. On your knees, wretch. I know the dreams which walk through your sleep. Repent and I shall change your punishment into grace. Don't be afraid for your innocence. There are many dwellings in God's mansion. You only need to open those amazing lips and the dove of our Lord will come flying and pour forth the Holy Spirit. It trembles with readiness, look. What is life without its daily death. You talk with angel's tongues. The school of the convent. The language of Mother Superior. Man should not spit out the gifts of God. To those who give it shall be given to them. What falls you should erect again. Christ would not have reached Golgatha without the righteous man who helped him carry the cross. Your hand, Madame. This is the resurrection. Did you say innocence. What you call your innocence is a blasphemy. He loves only ONE virgin, the world can do with one Saviour. Do you believe this eager body has been given to you so you can go to school alone, hidden from the eyes of the world. IT IS NOT GOOD THAT MAN SHALL BE ALONE. If you want to know where

God dwells trust the twitching of your thighs, the trembling of your knees. A tiny membrane should prevent us from becoming one body. THE PAIN IS SHORT BUT JOY WILL BE ETERNAL. He who brings the light should not be afraid of darkness: Paradise has three gates. He who rejects the third one insults the master-builder of the Trinity. THERE IS SPACE E'EN IN THE SMALLEST COTTAGE.

MERTEUIL You are very attentive, Sir. I am obliged to you since you have shown, could show, me so forcibly where God dwells. I won't forget any of His dwellings and take care that the flow of visitors doesn't stop and that His guests feel at home in them as long as I have breath to receive them.

VALMONT Why not a little longer. Breath should not be a condition of hospitality, death no grounds for divorce. Many a guest may have particular needs, LOVE IS AS STRONG AS DEATH. And let me do something more, my girl, whom I now may call woman. Woman has in the final outcome only one lover. I hear the clamour of battle, made by the clocks of the world which strike at your defenseless beauty. The thought that this glorious body will be exposed to the drapery in which the years enshroud it, that this mouth will shrivel, these breasts wither, this womb shrink under the plough of time, cuts so deeply into my soul that I want to assume the profession of the physician too, and help you to eternal life. I want to be the midwife of death, our mutual future. I want to fold my loving hands around your neck. How else can I pray for your youth with any prospect of success. I want to liberate your blood from the prison of veins, the bowels from the constraints of the body, the bones from the stranglehold of the flesh. How else can I grasp with my hands and see with my eyes what the transient shell hides from my view and my grasp. I want to release into the solitude of the stars the angel who dwells within you.

MERTEUIL The annihilation of the niece.

Pause.

MERTEUIL Shall we devour each other, Valmont, so this affair can come to an end before you become thoroughly tasteless.

VALMONT I regret having to tell you that I have dined already, Marchioness. The President's wife did fall.

MERTEUIL The eternal spouse.

VALMONT Madame de Tourvel.

MERTEUIL You are a whore, Valmont.

VALMONT I am expecting my punishment, Queen.

MERTEUIL Didn't my love for the whore deserve chastisement.

VALMONT I am dirt. I want to eat your excrement.

MERTEUIL Dirt to dirt. I want you to spit at me.

VALMONT I want you to urinate on me.

MERTEUIL Your excrement.

VALMONT Let us pray, Madame, that hell won't separate us.

MERTEUIL And now, Valmont, let us make the President's wife die of her futile fall from grace. Sacrificing the Queen.

VALMONT I have put myself at your feet, Valmont, so you won't stumble anymore. You have baptized me with the perfume of the gutter. From the heaven of my marriage I have thrust myself into the chasm of your desires in order to save this virgin. I have told you that I shall kill myself if you don't resist this time the evil that is reaching out from inside you. I have warned you, Valmont. All that is left for me to do is to include you in my final prayers. You are my murderer, Valmont.

MERTEUIL Am I. Too much honor, Madame. I have not decreed the commandments you wish to obey by executing yourself. Didn't you draw any pleasure from your pious adultery but that tender pang of conscience you are enjoying right now. You are not too cold for hell if I am to judge from our games in bed. No flesh under forty can lie as well as that. And what the rabble call suicide is the epitome of masturbation. You permit that I employ the aid of my lorgnette so I'll be able to watch better the performance—your last one, Queen—with fear and pity. I have had mirrors set up so you can die in the plural. And do me the favor: from my hands this your last glass of wine.

VALMONT I hope I shall be able to contribute to your amusement, Valmont, with this my last performance, since I cannot count on a moral effect after my belated glimpse at the slimy bottom of your soul. HOW TO GET RID OF THIS MOST WICKED BODY.* I shall open my veins as I would an unread book. You will learn how to read it, Valmont, after me. I shall do it with scissors since I am a woman. Every trade has its own jokes. You can use my blood to make yourself up, a new grimace. I shall find a way to my heart through my flesh. The way you never found, Valmont, since you are a man, your breast empty, and only nothingness growing inside you. Your body is the body of your death, Valmont. A woman has many bodies. You have to bleed yourself if you want to see blood. Or one man has to bleed the other. Envy of the milk in our breasts, that is what makes you men into butchers. If you only could give birth. I do regret, Valmont, that this experience will be denied you, this garden forbidden, because of a decree of nature hard to understand. You would give the best part of yourself for it if you knew what you

---

*English in the German text.

are missing and we could make a deal with nature. I did love you, Valmont. But I shall push a needle into my womb before I kill myself, to be sure nothing that you have planted is growing inside me, Valmont. You are a monster and I want to become one. Green and bloated with poison I shall walk through your sleep. Swinging from a rope I shall dance for you. My face will be a blue mask. The tongue protruding. With my head in the gas oven I will be aware that you are standing behind me with no thought but how to get inside me, and I, I will desire it while the gas bursts my lungs. It is good to be a woman, Valmont, and not a conqueror. When I close my eyes I can see you rotting. I don't envy you the cesspool growing inside you, Valmont. Do you want to know more. I am a dying encyclopedia, every word a clot of blood. You don't have to tell me, Marchioness, that the wine was poisoned. I wish I could watch you die as I watch myself now. By the way, I am still pleased with myself. This can masturbate even with the maggots. I hope my performance didn't bore you. That indeed would be unpardonable.

MERTEUIL Death of a whore. We are alone now cancer my lover.

END

Heartpiece

HEARTPIECE (*Herzstuck*), written 1981, was published in "Verlag der Autoren Programmheft," Nr. 9/81, Frankfurt/Main 1981, and first performed November 11, 1981, at the Bochum Theatre as part of a multi-space theatre event, "Unsere Welt" ("Our World") in the street before the theatre's main entrance. It was directed by the team Manfred Karge/Matthias Langhoff, who have staged various other Müller texts.

Two musicians, a pianist and a violinist, began to play a classical piece when suddenly they erupted in the dialogue of the playlet. This dialogue has the terseness and implies the broad gestures clowns employ when they perform in the circus ring. It can't but remind the reader of Brecht's "Clownspiel" ("Clownplay"), the interlude in his *Baden Play of Learning How to Agree*, in which a Mr. Schmidt—step by step—is amputated by two other clowns, until finally his head is taken off, and they leave him dying.

C.W.

ONE   TWO

ONE   May I put my heart at your feet.
TWO   As long as you don't
       soil my floor.

ONE   My heart is pure.
TWO   We'll see to that.

ONE   I can't get it out.
TWO   You'd like me to help you.

ONE   If you don't mind.
TWO   It's my pleasure.
       I too can't get it out.

ONE   CRIES.
TWO   I'll take it out by surgery.
       What do I have a penknife for.
       We'll get this in a minute.
       To work and not despair.
       Well, it's done.
       But this is a brick.
       Your heart is a brick.

ONE   But it beats only for you.

END

DESPOILED SHORE MEDEAMATERIAL LANDSCAPE WITH
ARGONAUTS, at Schauspielhaus, Vienna, 1983.

Despoiled Shore

Medeamaterial

Landscape with Argonauts

DESPOILED SHORE MEDEAMATERIAL LANDSCAPE WITH ARGO-
NAUTS (*Verkommenes Ufer Medeamaterial Landschaft mit Argonauten*) was
completed in 1982 and first published in *Theater Heute*, Nr. 6, Berlin 1983.
The first production was staged April 22, 1983, by Manfred Karge and Matthias
Langhoff, at the Bochum Theatre, a house that under the Artistic Direction of
Claus Peymann has become a kind of West German "home" for Heiner Müller: all
his recent plays have been performed at Bochum, some had their world premieres
there.

Müller constructed the text from newly written material and fragments of earlier
writings: "DESPOILED SHORE," he told *Der Spiegel* in an interview, "is thirty
years old except for a few lines . . . About half of the centerpiece, the Medea play,
is probably fifteen years old. Really new is the last segment only, LANDSCAPE
WITH ARGONAUTS." In the same interview Müller agreed with the interpretation that the text is autobiographical, that it isn't the traveller and conqueror Jason
who is speaking but Heiner Müller. However, he explained Jason's story as the
earliest myth of colonization in Greek legend: "The end signifies the threshold
where myth turns into history: Jason is slain by his boat . . . European history
began with colonization . . . That the vehicle of colonization strikes the colonizer
dead anticipates the end of it. That's the threat of the end we're facing, the 'end of
growth.' "

The play is indeed a "synthetic fragment": myth, history (the image of deserters
who have been hanged in the streets during the last weeks of World War II in Germany, for instance), very personal responses to contemporary realities ("Whatever
the subject is, I write in my contemporary context, for example about Colchis in the
GDR"), dreams remembered—all these elements are tied together in a complex
poetic structure. In its abundant imagery, the text is crammed with allusions,
literal and paraphrased quotes from Müller's own and other writings, splinters of
dreams and memories; a composite that challenges the reader's knowledge and imagination.

The first part, DESPOILED SHORE, evokes East Berlin suburbia with its lakes,
commuter trains, housing developments, etc., a polluted landscape swarming with
people whose minds are just as polluted. This "Despoiled shore, lake near
Straussberg" appeared already in the Kleist sequence of FREDERICK OF
PRUSSIA, though Kleist's suicide actually happened at the shore of another lake

near Berlin, the Wannsee, now in the Western part of the city. Obviously there is a connection indicated with the Prussian past of Berlin, and since Müller wrote most of this section thirty years earlier, we can assume that images of a "polluted" Prussian landscape had been on his mind for decades.

MEDEAMATERIAL stays close to the traditional Medea story, though it has become mainly a monologue of the betrayed-and-avenging-woman and mother, framed by two brief dialogue scenes of which the last consists of two lines only.

The final section, LANDSCAPE WITH ARGONAUTS, reads like and probably is based on a dream, the dream of a man's (the author's?) voyage across oceans and landscapes in their terminal state of pollution by technologies, art and war, ending with the extermination of the voyager who turns into a landscape, the landscape of his death. An end that evokes the image of an ultimate holocaust.

Müller puts a world on stage where warfare never stops. He once mentioned that all three parts of the text are "happening simultaneously," and he'd leave it to the theatre to arrive at the appropriate presentation.

C.W.

This text needs the naturalism of the stage. DESPOILED SHORE can be performed in a peep show, for example, as part of the regular presentation; MEDEAMATERIAL at a lake near Straussberg that is a muddy swimming pool in Beverly Hills or the baths of a psychiatric hospital. Just as MAUSER presumed a society of transgression in which a man condemned to death can turn his real death on stage into a collective experience, LANDSCAPE WITH ARGONAUTS presumes the catastrophes which mankind is working toward. The theatre's contribution to their prevention can only be their representation. The landscape might be a dead star where a task force from another age or another space hears a voice and discovers a corpse. As in every landscape, the I in this segment of the text is collective.

AUTHOR'S NOTE

DESPOILED SHORE

A lake near Straussberg Despoiled shore Tracks
Of flatheaded Argonauts
Reeds Dead branches
THIS TREE WILL NOT OUTGROW ME Dead fish
Gleam in the mud Cookie boxes Feces FROMMS ACT* CASINO**
The torn menstrual napkins The blood
Of the women of Colchis
BUT YOU MUST BE CAREFUL YES
YES YES YES YES
MUDCUNT I SAY TO HER THAT'S MY MAN
SCREW ME COME SWEETIE
Until the Argo crashes his skull the useless ship
That hangs in the tree Hangar and place for the dung of vultures in wait

They sit in the trains Faces made of the dailies and spit
Each one a naked member in his fly they stare at painted
Flesh Gutter that costs three weeks pay Till the coat of paint
Cracks Their wives keep the dinner warm air the bedding in the windows brush
The vomit out of their Sunday suits Waste pipes
Ejecting babies in batches against the advance of the maggots
Booze is cheap
The children piss in the empty bottles
Dream of an enormous
Coitus in Chicago
Women smeared with blood
In the morgues
The dead don't stare into the window
They are not drumming on the john

---

*Popular German brand of condoms.
**Cheap East German brand of cigarettes.

That's what they are Earth shat upon by the survivors
SOME WERE HANGING FROM LAMPPOSTS THEIR TONGUES PRO-
TRUDING

IN FRONT OF THE BELLY THE SIGN I AM A COWARD

Yet on the ground Medea cradling
The brother hacked up to pieces She expert
In poisons

MEDEAMATERIAL

MEDEA
Jason My first one and my last one Nurse
Where is my husband

NURSE
With Creon's daughter woman

MEDEA
Did you say with Creon

NURSE
With Creon's daughter

MEDEA
Did you say with Creon's daughter Yes
Why not with Creon's daughter who has power
Over her father Creon who alone
Can grant to us the right to live in Corinth
Or drive us out to other foreign shores
Right now perhaps he is embracing Jason
In supplication her unwrinkled knees
For me and for his sons whom he loves
Are you crying or laughing Nurse

NURSE
Lady I
Am older than my crying or my laughter

MEDEA
How are you living in your body's ruins
Together with the ghosts of your youth Nurse
Bring me a mirror This is not Medea
Jason

JASON
Woman what voice is this

MEDEA
I
Am not welcome here That death would reap me
It's three times five nights that you Jason didn't
Ask for me With this your voice you did not
And did not with a slave's voice nor
With hands nor with a glance

JASON
What do you want

MEDEA
Die

JASON
I've heard that often

MEDEA
Does this body
Mean nothing anymore to you Jason
Do you want to drink my blood

JASON
When will this end

MEDEA
When did it begin
Jason

JASON
What were you before I came woman

MEDEA
Medea
You owe me a brother Jason

JASON
Two sons I gave you for one brother

MEDEA
You Me Do you love them Jason your sons
Do you then want them back your sons
They're yours What can be mine being your slave
All of me is your tool and all things from me
For you I killed for you I did give birth
I've been your bitch your whore is what I was
I but a rung on your ladder of fame

Anointed with your feces your foes' blood
And if in memory of your victory
Over my country and my people that
Was my treason you want to make a wreath
From their entrails to adorn your temples
They're yours I own the images of those
Who have been slain the screams of all the tortured
Since I left Colchis left my home to follow
Your bloody tracks the blood of my own kind
Into my new and only home now treason
Blind to the images deaf to the screams
Was I until you tore the tightened net
Knitted of mine and of your lust
That was our home an alien country now
I stand disjointed in its mesh
The ashes of your kisses on my lips
Between my teeth the sand of our years
On my skin only my own sweat
Your breath a stench of alien bed
A man gives death in parting to his woman
My death it has no body now but yours
If you're my man then I am still your woman
Oh could I bite her out of you your whore
To whom you have betrayed me and my treason
That was your lust once Thanks for your treason
That gives me back both of my eyes again
To see what I saw once the images
You've painted with the boots of your crew Jason
Unto my Colchis ears to hear again
The music you once played upon the corpses
The bones the graves of those who were my people
With your crew's hands and with mine
Who was your bitch and who has been your whore
And my brother oh my brother Jason
Whom I threw unto your pursuers path
Dismembered he by these my sister hands
To help you to escape from our father
You'd robbed His father and mine Do you love
Your sons You want to have them back your sons
You still owe me a brother Jason
Whom do you love more Dog or bitch
When you gladeye your father and
Later his new bitch and the king
Of the dogs in Corinth here her father
Maybe your place is there then at his trough
Take Jason what you gave to me
The fruits of treason that grew from your seed

And stuff it into your whore's eager womb
My bridal present for your and her wedding
Go with your father who does love you So much
He kicks away your mother the barbarian
Who burdens you on your way to the top
Don't you want to sit at royal tables
I was the milkcow now I am your footstool
You'd like to Don't I see your eyes agleam
With the coming gladness of filled bellies
Why do you cling to the barbarian
Who is your mother and your blemish too
Actors you are the children of base treason
So sink your teeth into my heart and go
With your father who did the same before you
Leave me the children Jason one more day
And then I will go into my own desert
You still owe me a brother Jason
I can't hate for long what you love
Love comes and goes I wasn't prudent was I
Forgetting that No grudge shall be between us
Here take my bridal gown as bridal gift for
My lips can't say the word with ease your bride
Who will embrace your body Who will cry
On your shoulder will sometimes moan in heat
The gown of love my other skin
Embroidered by the hand of her who has been robbed
With gold from Colchis and dyed with the blood from
The bridal feast of fathers brothers sons
It shall adorn your new love just as if
It were my skin So I'll be close to you
Close to your love and far away from me
Go now to your new wedding Jason go
I'll turn the bride into a wedding torch
Watch your Mother stage a play for you
You want to see the new bride all aflame
The bridal gown of the barbarian has
The gift to weld an alien skin with death
Wounds and scars they make a splendid poison
The ash that was my heart is spewing fire
The bride is young Her hide is smoothly stretched
Not wasted yet by age nor any breeding
It's on her body that I write my play
I want to hear your laughter when she screams
Before midnight she will be all aflame
My sun will rise at Corinth's nightly sky
I want to see your laughter when it rises
And share my joy with you who are my children

The groom he enters now the bridal chamber
And now he places at the young bride's feet
The barbarian's bridal gown the bridal
Present soaked in my sweat of submission
Now see the whore she struts before the mirror
And now the gold of Colchis seals her pores
Planting a field of knives into her flesh
The barbarian's bridal gown it celebrates
Its wedding Jason of your virgin bride
The first night will be mine It is the last one
She screams now Have you ears to hear the scream
Like Colchis screamed when you were in my womb
And still screams Have you ears to hear the scream
She burns Hey laugh I want to see you laugh
My play it is a farce Why don't you laugh
What tears Tears for the bride My little ones
My traitors No you did not cry for nothing
I want to cut you right out of my heart
My heartflesh My remembrance My beloved
Give back to me my blood out of your veins
Back into my womb you who are my entrails
Today is payday Jason Your Medea
Will collect her debts today
Can you laugh now Death is but a present
And from my hands you shall receive the gift
I broke off forever all the bridges
To what I once called home Now I will do
The same for this my foreign shore with these
My human hands so it won't be a home
To you a mockery to me Alas
Would I'd remained the animal I was
Before my man made me into his woman
Medea The barbarian Now despised
With these my hands the hands of the barbarian
Well steeped in lye torn by the needle skinned
I want to break mankind apart in two
And live within the empty middle I
No woman and no man What do you scream
Worse than death is to grow old You'd kiss
The hand that gives you death if you knew life
That was Corinth Who are you Who has dressed
You in the bodies of my little children
What animal is hiding in your eyes
Do you play dead You won't deceive the mother
You're actors nothing but liars and traitors
Inhabited by dogs rats snakes you are
It barks it squeaks it hisses I can hear it

O I am wise I am Medea I
Don't you have blood left Now it is all quiet
The screams of Colchis silenced too And nothing left

JASON
Medea

MEDEA
Nurse Do you know this man

LANDSCAPE WITH ARGONAUTS

Shall I speak of me I who
Of whom are they speaking when
They do speak of me I Who is it
In the rain of bird droppings In the hide of lime
Or else I a banner a
Bloody rag hung out A fluttering
'Tween nothing and no one provided there is wind
I scum of a man I scum of
A woman Platitude piled on platitude I hell of dreams
Called by my accidental name I Fear of
My accidental name
MY GRANDFATHER WAS
AN IDIOT IN BOEOTIA
I my sea voyage
I my annexation My
Walk through the outskirts I My death
In the rain of bird droppings In the hide of lime
The anchor is the last umbilical cord
With the horizon the memory of the coast slips away
Birds are a farewell Are a reunion
The slaughtered tree it ploughs the snake the ocean
Thin between the I and the No more I the hull
SAILOR'S BRIDE IS THE SEA
The dead they say stand on the bottom
Upright swimmers Until the bones rest
Mating of fish in the corroded chest
Shoals of mussels on the skull
Thirst is fire
It is called water what burns the skin
Hunger chews the gums Salt the lips
Bawdry goads on the lonesome flesh
Until the man grabs for a man
Woman's warmth is a singsong

The stars are cold signposts
The sky an icy supervisor
Or the hapless landing Against the surf hisses
The pop of beer cans
FROM THE LIFE OF A MAN
Memory of a tank battle
My walk through the outskirts I
Between rubble and ruins it's growing
THE NEW Fuckcells with district heating
The tube vomits world into the livingroom
Wear and tear is part of the plan The container
Serves as a graveyard Figures among the rubble
Natives of the concrete Parade
Of Zombies perforated by TV spots
In the uniforms of yesterday morning's fashion
The youth of today ghosts of
The dead of the war that is to happen tomorrow
YET WHAT REMAINS IS CREATED BY BOMBS
In the splendid mating of protein and tin
The children lay out landscapes with trash
A woman is the familiar ray of hope
BETWEEN THE THIGHS
DEATH STILL HAS HOPE
Or the Yugoslavian dream
Among broken statues on the run
From an unknown catastrophe
The mother in tow the old one with her yoke
FUTURE in rusty armour travels along
A flock of actors passes in step
DON'T YOU NOTICE THEY ARE DANGEROUS THEY ARE
ACTORS EACH CHAIR LEG IS ALIVE A DOG
Wordmud from my
Abandoned no man's body
How to find the way out of the thicket
Of my dreams that slowly closes in
Without a sound around me
A shred of Shakespeare
In the paradise of the bacteria
The sky is just a glove gone hunting
Masked with clouds of an unknown type of architecture
Resting on the dead tree The corpses' sisters
My fingers play in the vagina
At the nightly window between city
And landscape we watched the flies dying slowly
As Nero stood exultant above Rome
Until the car drove up sand in the gearbox
A wolf stood in the street as the car fell apart
A bus ride in the early dawn right and left

The sisters steaming under dresses Noon
Sprinkled my hide with their ashes
During the ride we heard the screen rip
And watched the images crash into each other
The forests burned in EASTMAN COLOR*
But the voyage had no arrival NO PARKING*
At the only crossroads Polypheme
Controlled the traffic with his one eye
Our port was a dead movie house
On the screen the stars rotted in competition
In the lobby Fritz Lang strangled Boris Karloff
The Southern wind toyed with old posters
OR THE HAPLESS LANDING The dead negroes
Rammed into the swamp like poles
In the uniforms of their enemies
DO YOU REMEMBER DO YOU NO I DON'T*
The dried up blood
Is smoking in the sun
The theatre of my death
Had opened as I stood between the mountains
In the circle of dead comrades on the stone
And the expected airplane appeared above me
Without thinking I knew
This engine was
What my grandmothers used to call God
The airblast swept the corpses off the plateau
And shots crackled at my reeling flight
I felt MY blood come out of MY veins
And turn MY body into the landscape
Of MY death
                    IN THE BACK THE SWINE
The rest is poetry Who has the better teeth
The blood or the stone

                              END

---

*English in the original.

Since PAJ published my translation of Müller's text HAMLETMACHINE in 1980, I've encountered a nearly consistent set of responses to Müller's work, ranging from unmitigated enthusiasm to confusion and even disgust with his theatrical mode and the philosophy expressed in his texts. I had intended to discuss some of the misunderstandings and recurrent questions with Heiner Müller; however, the occasion for the planned interview failed to materialize. As the next best thing I mailed him a questionnaire containing the questions I am most frequently asked in context with his work. Needless to say that many of them wouldn't be my questions, and I was quite sure Heiner would regard some as naive, if not worse. Yet, I felt they should be dealt with to clarify some of the confusion surrounding his work. In his answers, he occasionally repeated statements he'd made previously in interviews or essays. He ignored a few questions, mainly those dealing with his present view of Brecht, and he added some, so he could elaborate on certain aspects. I find this composite of carefully phrased statements and quite spontaneous, often sarcastic, remarks an amusing introduction to Müller's witty and idiosyncratic mode of discourse.

C.W.

19 Answers by Heiner Müller

"I Am Neither a Dope—
Nor a Hope—Dealer"

A couple of years ago you were invited to a conference on Postmodernism in New York. You couldn't attend the conference but submitted a paper defining your position versus some aspects of contemporary art. Could you explain what in your opinion would constitute a Postmodern drama, a Postmodern theatre?

The only Postmodernist I know of was August Stramm, a modernist who worked in a post office.

Language takes a central position in your work, much more than it usually does in contemporary American drama. Could you explain what you feel language's function is in the contemporary theatre?

I would take issue with the premise in the first part of your question. Language is also important in American drama and other media but it is a different language, I think, with perhaps a different function. A film critic once asked me why stage and film productions in the GDR tend to use a poeticizing rather than what he called a naturalistic language, why the tendency toward stylization rather than realism. The extent to which that is valid comes from the fact that the GDR is not photographable, the fact that here actors cannot even say "Guten Tag" without it sounding like a lie. Realism doesn't work at all, only stylization works—a variation of Brecht's remark that a photograph of the Krupp Works says nothing really about the Krupp Works. The actors in the West are much better at Naturalism, at working with photographic texts or plays or films. Here they are better in productions of the classics, i.e., in anything that entails a stylized removal from immediate reality.

What is the role of language versus the rich visual imagery you employ to an ever increasing degree in your plays?

The worst experience I had during my stay in the United States was a film I saw called *Fantasia*, by Disney. I had never heard of it and actually ended up watching it by mistake. There were three films playing in the same movie house and I went into the wrong one. The most barbaric thing about this film, something I learned later, was that almost every American child between the ages of six and eight gets to view it. Which means that these people will never again be able to hear specific works by Beethoven, Bach, Handel, Tchaikovsky, etc., without seeing the Disney figures and images. The horrifying thing for me in this is the occupation of the imagination by clichés and images which will never go away; the use of images to prevent experiences, to prevent the having of experiences.

What has this got to do with your theatre?

Wolfgang Heise, a philosopher here in the GDR, once said that theatre is a laboratory for the social imagination. I find that relevant for what we are talking about. If one starts with the assumption that capitalist societies, indeed every industrial society, the GDR included, tends to repress and instrumentalize imagination—to throttle it—then for me the political task of art today is precisely the mobilization of imagination. To return to our example of *Fantasia*, the metaphorical function of the Disney film is to reduce the symbolic force of images to one meaning, to make them immediately allegorical. The imagery one finds in the early Russian cinema, on the other hand, is like the torrent of metaphors at the heart of Elizabethan literature. Here metaphors are constructed as a kind of visual protection against a much too rapidly changing reality, a reality that can only be dealt with and assimilated in this very special way. A world of images is created that does *not* lend itself to conceptual formulation and that cannot be reduced to a one-dimensional metaphor. This is what I try to do in my theatre.

You have written in other literary forms, poetry, short story, etc., but you always returned to the theatre, recently even as the director of your plays. Do you believe then that the theatre is a superior medium to investigate the complex problems of our time?

I have a real difficulty writing prose. I don't believe in literature as a work of art to be read. I don't believe in reading. I couldn't imagine writing a novel.

Where does your distrust of prose come from?

Writing prose you are all alone. You can't hide yourself. I also don't think I can write prose in the third person. I can't write: "Washington got up and went to 42nd Street." I can only imagine writing prose in the first person. Writing drama you always have masks and roles and you can talk through them. That's why I prefer drama—because of the masks. I can say one thing and say the contrary. I have a need to get rid of contradictions and that is easier to do with drama.

The theatre seems to have increasing difficulties in reaching wider audiences, larger sections of society, especially when it tries to interact with, or activate, its audiences. Where do you see reasons for this development and how should one cope with this danger of elitism?

This "elitism," as you call it, this not being immediately accessible, can also have its advantages. For accessibility is often connected with commercialization. Art becomes commercial at precisely the moment when its time is past. The tension between success and impact, which Brecht spoke of, is important in this respect: that one is always overtaken by success before a real impact can occur. As long as a thing works it is not successful, and when success is there then the impact is over. This is because there can only be an impact if, as for example in the theatre, the audience is split, brought home to its real situation. But that means there will be no agreement, no success. Success happens when everybody is cheering, in other words, when there is nothing more to say. For me the theatre is a medium which still permits one to avoid that kind of success. In film that is difficult because of the money involved.

But what about the GDR?

In our country, theatre allows you to have 500 or 800 people together in one room reacting at the same time, in the same space, to what is happening on stage. The impact of the theatre here is based on the absence of other ways of getting messages across to people. Films are not as important either because there is so much control. As a result, the theatre here has taken over the function of the other media in the West. I don't believe theatre has a great impact in West Germany, for instance. (We can forget about the United States.) You can do anything on the stage there but it doesn't mean anything to the society. Here the slogan of the Napoleonic era still applies: Theatre is the Revolution on the march.

In many of your texts you deal with topics which in this country would be defined as "feminist"; and female characters often have a central place in your work. Could you explain how you think women should be presented on the contemporary stage?

As a playwright I don't deal with "isms" but with reality. Can you tell me what a real female character is?

Your work is firmly rooted in history and/or mythology. American drama deals rarely with the past. What do you conceive as the function of mythology and history in the contemporary theatre?

The dead are in the overwhelming majority when compared to the living. And Europe has a wealth of dead stored up on that side of the ledger. The United States, not satisfied just with dead Indians, is fighting to close the gap. Literature, as an instrument of democracy, while not submitting to, should nevertheless be respectful of, majorities as well as of minorities.

Some of your critics maintain that at the center of your recent work is the conflict between the individual's desire "to pursue happiness" and the individual's responsibility to history and mankind's progress. Do you agree with this view? If yes, could you speak to this contradiction and its present manifestations?

"We Germans were not put here on earth to enjoy ourselves but to do our duty." (Bismarck)

If you disagree, what would you regard as a central issue in your recent texts?

How should I know, and if I knew why should I tell you?

If you reject this idea of a central issue, could you mention some of the interests you pursue in your writing?

See above.

Your plays have been performed in East and West Germany, in the United States, and in many other countries. You participated in many of these productions and recently have directed your plays in both Germanies. What difference could you observe in the theatrework of these different social and cultural systems, and what did they have in common?

To answer this question I am going to have to wait for more performances in East and West.

a) Where is the theatre, in your opinion, a more efficient instrument of social impact? b) Where would you prefer to direct, and to watch, your plays on stage?

a) In the East. b) I would like to stage MACBETH on top of the World Trade Center for an audience in helicopters.

There has been a lot of attention given to the so-called "New Subjectivity" in German letters, as exemplified by writers like Handke, Strauss, Laederach, etc. Do you see yourself in any relation to them and their work?

No. Nor do I see any relation of them to each other.

Terms like "Despair," "Pessimism," "Guilt," are often used by critics writing about your work. Do you think these are adequate definitions of your intentions and/or values?

Three times No.

People familiar with your recent texts often complain about a total lack of hope in your writing. What is your opinion?

I am neither a dope- nor a hope- dealer.

Would you care to comment on your views about the future of our world which you paint so darkly in your work?

The future of the world is not my future.
"Show me a mousehole and I'll fuck the world." (Railworker at the soft-coal strip mine Klettwitz, GDR.)

PAJ PLAYSCRIPTS

GENERAL EDITORS: Bonnie Marranca and Gautam Dasgupta